Terry Power

D1235367

THE GOSPEL CONVERSATIONAL CHURCH

CULTIVATING
A CULTURE
OF ENGAGING
IN GOSPEL
CONVERSATIONS

Sam Greer

WESTBOW
PRESS®
A DIVISION OF THOMAS NELSON
& ZONDERVAN

WestBow Press books may be ordered through booksellers or by contacting:

WestBow Press
A Division of Thomas Nelson & Zondervan
1663 Liberty Drive
Bloomington, IN 47403
www.westbowpress.com
1 (866) 928-1240

Scripture quotations are from the ESV® Bible (The Holy Bible, English Standard Version®), copyright © 2001 by Crossway, a publishing ministry of Good News Publishers. Used by permission. All rights reserved.

ISBN: 978-1-9736-8145-8 (sc)
ISBN: 978-1-9736-8146-5 (hc)
ISBN: 978-1-9736-8144-1 (e)

Library of Congress Control Number: 2019920252

Print information available on the last page.

WestBow Press rev. date: 12/12/2019

Contents

Foreword vii

Dedication ix

Introduction xi

Chapter 1   Making the Great Commission Great Again 1

Chapter 2   Missing the Mode of Everyday Evangelism 36

Chapter 3   Ignoring Your Oikos is not Okay 48

Chapter 4   Focusing on the Wrong List 63

Chapter 5   Turning From Avoiding Gospel Conversations 79

Chapter 6   Talking About Gospel Conversations 86

Chapter 7   Teaching a Gospel Conversational Tool 98

Chapter 8   Targeting a Goal for Gospel Conversations 109

Chapter 9   Training People to Have Gospel Conversations..........115

Chapter 10 Tracking the Progress of Gospel Conversations......... 120

End Notes 129

Foreword

It's a very encouraging time when I pick up the book such as I am commending you now on the great commission. It is so encouraging to see a young pastor coming behind me that understands what making disciples is all about. Sam has used his giftedness as a writer to remind all of us in the Church of how we can make the great commission great again. Chapter one is worth the price of this book. You could place this in the hands of a missions committee or in a group that you're trying to connect their heart with our Heavenly Father's heart for the nations and they would get it very quickly.

Sam continues in his book by helping us realize that the light that shines the furtherest shines the brightest at home. How we do every day evangelism where we live to make sure we're not attempting to transport, that we do not possess in our local community.

I believe your people would thank you time and time again for placing this Christ honoring book in their hands. There is so much talk today about how to turn ordinary everyday conversation into gospel conversations. You will find that illustrated and you will find wonderful encouragement along with instructions on how to make this happen day in and day out. This is a how to book. It's a tool, a help for that church, that Pastor, that group of lay people that want to be faithful making Christ known in their Jerusalem, Judea, Samaria, and the uttermost parts of the earth.

You literally could use this book as a training manual for the great commission, our people desire to get it, to understand, to embrace the new testament model of making disciples. Let Sam Greer use his experience, his story of what's happened at Red Bank Baptist Church to make a difference in your church and literally to make a difference around the world. I encourage you to read this book then place it in the hands of those that will join you in the journey of making much of Jesus daily and for eternity.

Johnny Hunt
Senior Vice President of Evangelism and Pastoral Leadership
North American Mission Board, SBC

Dedication

To my wife Tonya, you are my Boo Boo and I love you.

To Braydee and Belle, may the most important relationship in your lives be with the Lord Jesus Christ.

To Bonner Creek Baptist Church, Hebron Baptist Church, Red Bank Baptist Church, and The Point Church, each of you took a chance on this Southern Mississippi boy and I am eternally grateful. May God continue to build His church!

Introduction

Does the local church really matter? In Matthew 16:18, Jesus said to Peter, "And I tell you, you are Peter and on this rock I will build my church, and the gates of hell shall not prevail against it." Jesus made it crystal clear that death itself would never prevail against His church, not even His own death.

Meanwhile, far too many people are tweeting, posting, hash-tagging, and throwing rotten eggs at the church. In fact, Red Bank Baptist Church once had a reputation in our own city, Chattanooga, TN, of being *Dead Bank* Baptist Church. Is the local church dead? Is the local church dying? Does God merely call local church pastors to officiate the funerals of local churches? Dr. Chuck Herring asked the question in a different way:

> Hey, millennials may say that the church is not relevant. Busy parents may say that they don't have time for the church. Liberals may say the church is dead. Scoffers say the church is full of hypocrites. Let me ask you a question: Are all of these people smarter than Jesus?[1]

Does the local church still matter to Jesus? Should the local church still matter to us?

In 2019 the Southern Baptist Convention was held in Birmingham, AL. Local reporters estimated a crowd of ten to fifteen thousand Southern Baptists who were expected to have an eighteen million dollar economic impact. Several highlights from the 2019 SBC were impactful, including: (1) over 300 Birmingham residents came to personal faith in Jesus Christ via gospel conversations had by Southern Baptists, (2) $250,000 was given by Southern Baptists to the mayor of Birmingham for the purpose of buying school supplies for children all over the city, and (3) one Alabama bi-vocational pastor's mortgage was paid off by the North American Mission Board.

One of the more personal highlights came on the morning of the second day. Our Red Bank Baptist Church staff and spouses, who were in attendance, had breakfast together and headed over to the business session for a very important vote, perhaps the most important vote in recent years: that is, a vote to approve the Committee on Nominations Report. How exciting, right? Sure, the SBC Messengers vote on this report every year at the convention. So, what was so special about this report? In short, my name was included in the report!

The Committee on Nominations Report includes all the Trustee nominations for all SBC entities. The International Mission Board Trustees were included, and I was one of the pastors nominated to be a Trustee. Serving on the IMB Trustee Board is my first opportunity to serve as a part of an SBC entity, and I am excited.

The SBC way of voting can be summed up by the words "raise your ballots." More specifically, "All in favor of the Committee on Nominations Report raise your ballots. Thank you. Any in opposition, raise your ballots. Thank you." The voting process seems simple enough. On our way over to the business session I asked all of our staff and spouses, "Do you have your ballots?" Everyone affirmed they had their ballot in their hand except for one, my wife Tonya. Tonya responded, "I can't get my ballot out of my purse because I just painted my nails and they are still wet. Can you get it for me?"

Soon after we took our seats in the general session, President J.D. Greear called for the vote to affirm the report by saying, "All in favor of affirming the report raise your ballots." We all raised our ballots. Well, at least, almost all of us raised our ballots. Tonya was fumbling around with her ballot, because, of all things, her nails were still wet, and she missed the opportunity to vote for the report.

Then it happened. After calling for votes in favor of the report, President Greear said, "Any in opposition to the report, raise your ballots." In a room of thousands of people, one ballot shot up in the air at that very moment, Tonya's ballot. After fumbling with her ballot, Tonya was somehow able, even with wet nails, to gain her composure and lift her ballot up in the air at the exact moment those in opposition were asked to raise their ballots. By voting against the motion, Tonya voted against me! That's right, she not only didn't vote *for* me, she voted *against* me! I love my wife, and she matters to me.

Even when we fumble around and miss this gospel opportunity or that one, Jesus loves His bride, the local church, and we matter to Him. Although the SBC is made up of over 46,000 churches and 15.74 million members, at each SBC gathering, I am reminded of the importance of each local church.

Some will continue to ask the question, *"Does the local church really matter?"* Without question, the local church matters to Jesus and she should matter to us as well. Yes, Jesus loves His bride and so should we. How do we know that the local church matters to Jesus?

Being the church matters to Jesus.

When Jesus and His disciples came into Caesarea Philippi, Jesus asked the question, "Who do people say that the Son of man is?" Then, his disciples gave him a "Who's Who" list of people; however, the identity of Jesus can't be decided by taking a *poll of people*. You can only decide the identity of Jesus by looking at *the pole for people*, that is, the pole upon which Jesus died. So, Jesus asked His disciples a follow-up question, "But who do you say that I am?"

Jesus didn't simply ask His disciples, "Who do you assume I am, believe I am, conclude I am, deduce I am, guesstimate I am, figure I am, hash-tag I am, hope I am, imagine I am, or think I am?" Jesus asked them, "Who do you *say* I am?" Jesus was ready to see what they were ready to say about him. Being the church is synonymous with confessing Jesus. Being the church is synonymous with having gospel conversations. Being the church matters to Jesus.

Blessing the church matters to Jesus.

Upon hearing Peter's confession that Jesus was "the Christ the Son of the living God," Jesus said, "Blessed are you Simon Bar-Jonah."

Why was Peter blessed? Peter was blessed because his gospel confession followed his gospel conversion, which came through gospel revelation from God the Father. Jesus still blesses His church in a similar way as gospel confession always follows gospel conversion, which happens through gospel conversations. Blessing the church matters to Jesus.

Building the church matters to Jesus.

Jesus didn't say to Peter, "*You* will build *your* church" or "*I* will build *your* church" or "*You* will build *my* church." Jesus said, "*I* will build *my* church." In a word, ouch! Fellow disciples of Christ, spoiler alert: Jesus doesn't need us. He wants us, but He doesn't need us. Frankly, Jesus is not interested in building our ministries. Jesus is only interested in building His church through His disciple's gospel confession about Him. Based on the Bible, Jesus is building gospel conversational churches through gospel conversations.

Jesus affirmed that upon the gospel confession of Peter and others, He would build His church. Furthermore, Jesus has promised that He will build His church based on the gospel confession of all His followers. Jesus builds His church by building people, not peopling buildings. Gospel conversations are the vehicles God uses to bring about gospel conversions that result in gospel confessions. As Jesus continues to make all things new, praise Him that gospel conversations never lose that new car smell! Building the church matters to Jesus.

Being the church, blessing the church, and building the church all matter to Jesus. Jesus will build His church, including any and every local church that chooses to yield to His will. What must we do to yield to Jesus' will? We must get serious about cultivating a culture of having gospel conversations. We must get serious about obeying the Great Commission. We must get serious about seeing local churches transformed from *good conservational churches* to *gospel conversational churches!*

The purpose of this book is to help the local church cultivate a culture of engaging in gospel conversations. Fulfilling the Great Commission is our mission. Fulfilling the Great Commission will never happen unless gospel conversations are happening. I am praying, have been praying, and will continue to pray for a gospel conversational movement in our churches, communities, convention, and country.

Will you join me in praying for a gospel conversational movement? Will you join me in asking God to allow your church to be a part of a gospel conversational movement? Are you ready to help cultivate a culture of engaging in gospel conversations in your church? Are you ready for your church to become a gospel conversational church? If so, then read on!

CHAPTER I

Making the Great Commission Great Again

"When asked if they had previously 'heard of the Great Commission,' half of U.S. churchgoers (51%) say they do not know this term."[2] – *Barna Group*

The 5 Great Commissions

How many sermons have you heard? How many sermons have you forgotten? The distance between those two numbers is certainly small as only a fraction of what goes in one ear does not go out the other ear. Jesus' disciples heard many sermons, parables, life lessons, truths, take-aways, and messages from Jesus. Doubtless they heard any like the one they heard after Jesus rose from the dead. Below is a helpful analogy concerning the depth of the attentiveness with which the disciples listened to Jesus in His resurrected state as written by Mark Corbett:

> Imagine that one Friday morning you were watching your preacher cross the street and – wham! – he got ran over by a speeding dump truck. When you reached him he was, beyond all doubt, dead. Your church quickly buries him.

You show up Sunday morning with a heavy heart, wondering who will speak and what they might say. And then, to your surprise and wonder, your preacher, with the tread marks still visible, walks up to the pulpit. Whatever he spoke about that Sunday morning, you would never forget it.

Of course, this is similar to what the disciples experienced. And what did Jesus talk about in this very memorable circumstance? The Great Commission.[3]

In Corbett's analogy, could we not agree that whatever this said resurrected pastor spoke about on that Sunday morning would never be forgotten? Don't you imagine that what Jesus said in that unforgettable moment in His resurrected body would have never been forgotten by His followers? Yet, tragically, when asked if they had "heard of the Great Commission," 51% of U.S. churchgoers said they don't even know the term. What's more, 25% say that the Great Commission "rings a bell" while only 17% of U.S. churchgoers know what the Great Commission is exactly.[4]

How is it that the unforgettable Great Commission is all but forgotten? The unforgettable Great Commission being forgotten is unacceptable. We must commit to making the Great Commission great again! Where do we start?

Five passages given by Jesus to His followers in the New Testament are considered part of the Great Commission.

Great Commission Biblical Reference	Great Commission Text	Great Commission Emphasis
Matthew 28:18-20	"And Jesus came and said to them, 'All authority in heaven and on earth has been given to me. Go therefore and make disciples of all nations, baptizing them in the name of the Father and of the Son and of the Holy Spirit, teaching them to observe all that I have commanded you. And behold, I am with you always, to the very end of the age.'"	Make disciples who Make disciples who Make disciples who...... Baptism Model discipleship by teaching others to observe all that Jesus commanded
Mark 16:15-16	"And he said to them, 'Go into all the world and proclaim the gospel to the whole creation. Whoever believes and is baptized will be saved, but whoever does not believe will be condemned."	Proclaim the gospel to all the world Baptism

Luke 24:45-49	"Then he opened their minds to understand the Scriptures, and said to them, Thus it is written, that the Christ should suffer and on the third day rise from the dead, and that repentance and forgiveness of sins should be proclaimed in his name to all nations, beginning from Jerusalem. You are witnesses of these things. And behold, I am sending the promise of my Father upon you. But stay in the city until you are clothed with power from on high."	Gospel conversations Engage in gospel conversations by offering an explanation of the gospel and extending an invitation to trust Jesus as Savior and follow Him as Lord Wait for Holy Spirit Empowered by the Spirit Be Jesus in your Jerusalem

John 20:21-23	"As the Father has sent me, even so I am sending you.' And when he had said this, he breathed on them and said to them, 'Receive the Holy Spirit. If you forgive the sins of any, they are forgiven them; if you withhold forgiveness from any, it is withheld.'"	Sent out by Jesus Empowered by the Holy Spirit The unforgiven can be forgiven The forgiven must forgive
Acts 1:8	"But you will receive power when the Holy Spirit has come upon you, and you will be my witnesses in Jerusalem and in all Judea and Samaria, and to the end of the earth."	We are witnesses Empowered by the Holy Spirit Missions

Before we unpack each of these Great Commission passages and their respective imperatives listed above, let's consider two churches who decided change was necessary to be a Great Commission church.

You are a part of our history; we want to be a part of your future.

Red Bank Baptist Church was established in 1911. Through the 1970s and '80s, Red Bank was a cutting edge church; it was one of the first in the area to launch an orchestra and a singles ministry. With a strong and rich history, I knew that Red Bank Baptist needed a fresh, new vision and would settle for nothing less. Upon my arrival in 2012 as the new Senior Pastor, I began to pray and ask God for a fresh vision.

Over time God revealed His vision for Red Bank through John 21:6: "Cast the net on the right side of the boat, and you will find some." The catch of fish was so large that the Bible even gives it a number, 153. The number *153* jumped off the page because one of the main highways in Chattanooga is Highway 153. Praying through that passage and thinking about how Red Bank Baptist could impact the city of Chattanooga with the gospel, God laid on my heart a multi-site church model. Although God made the multi-site model vision clear, it would not come to fruition for five more years.

The first step in seeing the vision become a reality was for our main campus to get healthy. We were sending upwards of 20% of all dollars coming into the church out to missions. That seems great at first glance, but our church campus in Red Bank was being neglected. No renovations had occurred in thirty to forty years.

Moving toward a more healthy church, we survived leading the church from thirty-three designated funds down to four: (1) World Missions Offering, (2) Benevolence, (3) Budget, and (4) Building. Then, in 2015, we entered into a three-year 2.5 million dollar renovation of our Worship Center and children's space, even paying it off early. Meanwhile, I was looking at every piece of available property in Hamilton County to purchase in order to launch a new site. God closed every door - until He didn't.

Making a routine hospital visit early on Wednesday, July 25, 2018, was anything but routine. The husband of the wife I was there to visit made the following statement: "I heard that Signal Mountain Baptist Church may be interested in selling their property." Signal Mountain is a nearby advantageous area where some of our members already live. In 1998, Signal Mountain Baptist was averaging over 400 in worship attendance, but by 2018 attendance dropped to around 60. Upon leaving the hospital, I rallied our pastors for a meeting.

We made one phone call, and it happened to be the contact person for the Signal Mountain Baptist Church Leadership Team. A meeting was scheduled for us to meet with their leadership. In preparation for our meeting, we discovered that Red Bank Baptist helped plant Signal Mountain Baptist in 1946. Sitting before the leadership team of Signal Mountain, God led me to say: "You are a part of our history; we want to be a part of your future."

From that point, the ball started moving down the field. Both churches voted to enter into what the SBC calls a strategic merger. Signal Mountain voted to dissolve and be acquired by Red Bank Baptist Church. Signal Mountain Baptist paid off the last of their debt on a twenty-year-old 750-seat Worship Center, and they wrote Red Bank Baptist a check at the official closing.

All the while, I am thinking that for us to launch a new site, it will cost millions. Literally, it cost Red Bank Baptist zero dollars to acquire this campus. We officially launched The Point Church at Signal on Palm Sunday 2019.

We sent 100 members of Red Bank Baptist, who committed to serve for one year, to the Signal campus. On Easter 2019, over 500 people worshiped at The Point Church and after about a year time frame average weekly attendance is right at 300. While some strategic mergers take anywhere from one to two years, the strategic merger between Red Bank Baptist and Signal Mountain Baptist took a couple of months.

The question I am asked most often about this strategic merger is this, "How did y'all do it?" My answer is always the same, "We didn't do it; God did it!" God decided to strategically merge two churches for His glory.

Even the North American Mission Board contacted us to affirm the validity of this merger. NAMB is having difficulty with smaller churches who enter into a two-year journey to merge with a larger church, but at the last minute the smaller church backs out. NAMB's purpose in contacting us was to hear the story of what it took for Signal Mountain Baptist to surrender to a strategic merger. In other words, NAMB has plenty of churches willing to help struggling churches, but the struggling churches struggle to surrender.

So, what led to Signal Mountain Baptist's willingness to surrender? In 2016, Signal Mountain Baptist formed a vision team who devoted themselves to prayer for two years. The vision team concluded that the best solution for their future was to merge with another church. While Signal Mountain Baptist was praying, God was preparing Red Bank Baptist to be healthy enough to send out 100 people for the launch of The Point Church at Signal, formerly Signal Mountain Baptist Church.

Cultivating a gospel conversational culture at Red Bank Baptist was critical to this merger becoming a reality. Yes, strategically casting a Great Commission vision over a five to six-year period took patience and time, but it was worth it. Preaching expository sermons with a steady diet of Great Commission fulfillment and gospel conversational focus was key. Sharing personal gospel conversation failures, not just victories, with staff and the church individually, in small groups, and collectively was also essential.

True "buy-in" only came after the church began to trust the leadership to do what the leadership said it would do. For example, "buy-in" on engaging in everyday evangelism only happened when the church saw the leadership having gospel conversations, not just talking about having gospel conversations. In a word, church leaders can't expect the church to do what they are unwilling to do.

Through this process, I have learned both that God knows what He is doing and that He is doing it. I also learned that to lead people, you must love them, and to love people, you must lead them. More specifically, when it comes to cultivating a gospel conversational church, I have learned that when people have Jesus on their mind, "Jesus" will come out of their mouth. As pastors and leaders, our job is to get Jesus on their mind and to teach them ways to ensure that Jesus stays on their mind. Preach Jesus!

One helpful approach that will cultivate a gospel conversational culture in your church is to highlight the Great Commission passages in the New Testament. Each of these five sections below deals with one aspect of the Great Commission Emphasis noted in the aforementioned Great Commission graph.

May God bless you as you seek to cultivate a gospel conversational culture in your ministry context by making the Great Commission great again.

1. Great Commission According to Mark and Matthew

Be Biblically Baptized

> "Whoever believes and is *baptized* will be saved, but whoever does not believe will be condemned." Mark 16:16

> "...*baptizing* them in the name of the Father and of the Son and of the Holy Spirit..." Matthew 28:19

Followers of Jesus must follow Jesus in biblical baptism. The early church model of publicly professing faith in Christ Jesus was through the ordinance of biblical baptism. Any other formal way of professing faith in Christ publicly is foreign to the New Testament. We are to be biblically baptized. We are not to be traditionally baptized, denominationally baptized, or even Babylon Bee baptized.

An article from the Christian satirical news source, *The Babylon Bee*, entitled **"Man's Baptism Overturned After Instant Replay Reveals He Was Not Fully Submerged"** reported that after a baptismal candidates finger was above the water while being baptized church officials reviewed the video and concluded: "Incomplete submersion by the offense, conversion overturned. 12-month penalty serving in children's ministry," the officials declared as the crowd booed. "Salvation denied."[5]

We are not to be Babylon Bee baptized, but biblically baptized. Yet, far too many folks in the American church refuse to follow through in obedience to Jesus' command of being baptized. So-called "Christians" claim to have placed their faith alone, by grace alone, in Christ alone, but treat baptism as an insignificant matter that doesn't matter.

In the American church, we have fashioned a Jesus *after us*, rather than us coming *after Jesus*. We have fashioned a Jesus who doesn't *make demands of us*, but a Jesus who *makes concessions for us*. We have fashioned a Jesus who isn't *like no other*, but a Jesus who is *like us*. We have fashioned a Jesus of *little us'*, rather than a Jesus who is *Lord over us*. As Pastor Micah Fries has said, "A Jesus of our own fashioning is everywhere in the Bible Belt and nowhere in the Bible."[6]

This erroneous and disobedient line of thinking bleeds over into baptism. Is baptism of little consequence? Has Jesus left the decision of whether or not to be baptized up to the individual? Or, has Jesus already spoken on the issue of obedience through baptism for every follower of Christ?

Did Jesus really say, *"All authority* in heaven and on earth has been given to me. Go therefore and make disciples of all nations *baptizing them…."*? Did Jesus really mean *all* authority or *some* authority? Does Jesus really mean what He says and say what He means?

When it comes to the Great Commission, how important is biblical baptism? What does the ordinance of baptism have to do with cultivating a gospel conversational culture? The following seven questions may be helpful in discovering the importance of biblical baptism in the life of a gospel conversational church.

Is baptism a matter of ignorance? For some, the reluctance they have toward being baptized may be a matter of ignorance. Ignorance is not synonymous with stupidity. Ignorance is about being *uninformed,* not *unintelligent.*

According to Acts 17:30, "The times of ignorance God overlooked, but now he commands all people everywhere to repent." Consider yourself informed that you are no longer uninformed or ignorant of what God expects of you.

In Acts 2:38, Peter preached at Pentecost, "Repent and be baptized every one of you…" After the initial repentance, the first step of obedience for any new believer is baptism. Jesus' followers must follow Him in biblical baptism.

What is biblical baptism? Biblical baptism is baptism by immersion. The meaning of the Greek New Testament word "baptizo" is "to plunge, dip, submerge in water."[7] Baptism by sprinkling or by pouring, therefore, is self-contradictory as it is impossible to plunge, dip or submerge someone in water by sprinkling water on them. The New Testament leaves no room for any other mode of baptism other than baptism by immersion.

A gospel conversational church is one which unapologetically calls each Christ-follower, whether he or she is a new believer or a long-time believer, to follow Jesus in biblical baptism. Part of the discipleship process is teaching believers the importance of biblical baptism.

Pastors and leaders must never assume that all believers understand baptism or that they have been biblically baptized. Part of cultivating a gospel conversational culture is making a big deal about a believer's salvation by celebrating his or her public baptism.

Ignorance on the matter of baptism must no longer be ignored!

Is baptism a matter of indifference? Jesus took and takes baptism so seriously that He was baptized so that His followers could follow Him in biblical baptism. Yet, for some people, refusing baptism is a matter of indifference as they simply don't see the value of being baptized. How significant was Jesus' baptism?

In Matthew 3:16-17, the Bible says, "And when Jesus was baptized, immediately he went up from the water, and behold, the heavens were opened to him, and he saw the Spirit of God descending like a dove and coming to rest on him; and behold, a voice from heaven said, 'This is my beloved Son, with whom I am well pleased.'" Let it not be lost on us that Jesus' baptism was so significant that all three Persons of the Trinity showed up: God the Father, God the Son and God the Holy Spirit.

Do you realize that God the Son so pleased God the Father that at His baptism the Father audibly spoke from heaven? Do you realize that each time a follower of Christ follows Jesus in baptism that God the Father is pleased? How is it that God is pleased with followers of Jesus who follow Jesus in baptism?

When anyone places their faith alone, by grace alone, in Jesus alone, God the Father is pleased. Furthermore, when that new follower of Christ follows Jesus in baptism, God looks on him or her and says that this is My son or My daughter with whom I am well pleased. Understand, as followers of Jesus, God's pleasure with us is not based on how well we did today or yesterday, but how well Jesus did when He lived, died, and was raised again. God *can* be pleased with us because He *is* pleased with Jesus.

Why, then, are we so ready to dismiss, discount, disregard, discard, dispose of, dispense with, or be indifferent toward the one public act, baptism, that we know pleases God the Father? Why are we being indifferent toward baptism, which is the one public act that demonstrates you were made different by the one, Jesus, who makes all the difference?

Be different by no longer being indifferent toward baptism!

Is baptism a matter of arrogance? While reluctance to being baptized may be a matter of ignorance or indifference for some, for others baptism is a matter of arrogance. The biblical order of baptism follows conversion. Too many people were baptized at a young age and trusted Christ at a later age. In such cases, the problem, of course, is that their baptism is out of order; their baptism is on the wrong side of salvation. Rather than push pride aside and obediently submit to biblical baptism, some give in to the temptation of arrogantly, claiming they have already been baptized.

Luke, in Acts 8:12, clearly communicates the biblical order of salvation and baptism, "But when they believed Philip as he preached the good news about the kingdom of God and the name of Jesus Christ, they were baptized, both men and women." First, Philip preached the good news. Second, the people heard the good news. Third, they believed the good news. Fourth, they were baptized. The biblical order is not *be baptized and believe*, but *believe and be baptized*.

In the second church God led me to pastor, Hebron Baptist Church, I preached a sermon on biblical baptism. After calling people to get their baptism in order, an invitation was extended. One of the first people who responded to the invitation was my wife, Tonya. Tonya was baptized at a young age but trusted in Jesus in her teenage years. Her baptism was out of order. Talk about overcoming pride, the pastor's wife presented herself for baptism and many others followed suit.

Obedience is contagious! You never know who God has prepared to push pride aside and follow Jesus when you obediently lead the way. Have you believed the good news about Jesus? Have you been biblically baptized? If not, why not? Is your baptism in order or out of order?

Push pride aside by no longer allowing baptism to be a matter of arrogance!

Is baptism a matter of defiance? For some, the reluctance toward being baptized is a matter of outright defiance. The idea of being defiant and refusing baptism is a foreign concept in the New Testament. Why would anyone be defiant toward biblical baptism? Two common examples of people who may refuse biblical baptism are those who have been sprinkled at some point or baptized as infants.

After Peter preached at Pentecost, the Bible says, in Acts 2:41, "So those who received His Word were baptized." The Bible doesn't read "some of those who received His Word refused baptism" but "those who received His Word were baptized." The Scripture suggests that the people were obediently following Peter's instructions to *repent and be baptized*.

So, who is it that can receive God's Word? Can an infant receive God's Word? An infant is unable to receive God's Word and repent; therefore, infant baptism is not biblical baptism. Biblical baptism is an outward expression of an inward change. The only way an infant can experience change is by way of a new diaper. Infants can't be changed because they are unable to receive God's Word and repent.

Thomas P. Johnston shared a helpful comparison between the Roman Catholic and mainstream Protestant view of infant baptism and the Baptist view of biblical baptism. He wrote, "The Roman or mainstream Protestant order generalizes the particularity of baptism, while reversing the emphasis of those who should evangelize. The Roman or mainstream Protestant view is as follows:

○ Baptism of all infants (generalized)
○ Evangelizing is only for ordained clergy (particularized).

The Baptist view, however, opposes this understanding:

○ Baptism is only for professing disciples (particularized).
○ Evangelizing is for all professing disciples (generalized, among the saved)."[8]

While pastoring Bonner Creek Baptist Church, the first church God called me to pastor, one of the leaders in the church said, "Pastor, I grew up in the Catholic Church, and I promised my momma on her death bed that I would never be baptized by immersion." With all due respect to all mothers, mother-in-laws, and momma & dems, momma is not Lord: Jesus is Lord!

Follow Jesus in biblical baptism by no longer allowing baptism to be a matter of defiance!

Is baptism a matter of resemblance? Certainly, baptism is a matter of resemblance as it is a picture of the death, burial, and resurrection of

Jesus. A follower of Christ follows Jesus in baptism for the purpose of identifying with Him in His death, burial, and resurrection. How do we know that baptism helps us identify with Christ in this way?

Paul wrote in Romans 6:3-4: "Do you not know that all of us who have been baptized into Christ Jesus were baptized into his death? We were buried therefore with him by baptism into death, in order that, just as Christ was raised from the dead by the glory of the Father, we too might walk in newness of life."

The only mode of baptism capable of capturing the death, burial and resurrection of Christ is baptism by immersion. When one is immersed under the water the burial of Christ is pictured. Coming up out of the water symbolizes the resurrection of Christ. Any other mode of baptism is incapable of resembling Christ's death, burial, and resurrection, that is, the gospel of Jesus.

I have yet to attend a funeral where the funeral director took a cup full of dirt and threw it on top of the casket and said, "Okay, your loved one is buried." You can no more be buried with Christ by sprinkling a cup of water on your head, than you can bury a loved one by throwing a cup of dirt on top of his or her casket. Why would you want to be baptized any other way, but the one way that pictures the good news of Jesus which saved you in the first place?

Follow Jesus in biblical baptism because baptism resembles the good news of Jesus' death, burial and resurrection!

Is baptism a matter of significance? All of the Scriptures mentioned already aid in establishing the significance of baptism. Questions surrounding the extent of the significance of baptism still remain. Just how significant is baptism? Does baptism save? Does the Bible teach baptismal regeneration?

In 1 Corinthians 1:14 and 17, Paul wrote:

I thank God that I baptized none of you except Crispus and Gaius, so that no one may say that you were baptized in my name....For Christ did not send me to baptize but to preach the gospel, and not with words of eloquent wisdom, lest the cross of Christ be emptied of its power.

Paul made it clear that God sent him for the purpose of preaching the gospel. If baptism played any part in a person being saved, then don't you imagine Paul and all the apostles would have baptized everyone? Baptism saves no one, but the gospel can save anyone. Is baptism significant? Yes! Does baptism save? No! Baptism is an outward demonstration of an inward regeneration. Salvation is by grace alone, through faith alone, in Christ alone.

Be careful not to make baptism more or less than what God intended!

Is baptism a matter of obedience? At Pentecost, Peter preached a simple gospel message by identifying Jesus as Lord and claiming that all who call upon Jesus will be saved. This, Peter's first sermon, was his best sermon as 3,000 people were saved, the promised Holy Spirit arrived, and the church was born. As a pastor, I almost feel sorry for Peter in that his best sermon was his first sermon. Apparently, it was all downhill for Peter, the preacher, after Pentecost.

Coming to the realization that Jesus is Lord means there is only one thing left to do: repent and be baptized. Baptism can't be a matter of convenience, it must be a matter of obedience. Dr. Chuck Herring wrote, "I must say that, as I have studied my Bible, it certainly seems that the American church has made baptism a matter of convenience instead of a matter of obedience."[9]

Forsake your disobedience by no longer allowing baptism to be a matter of convenience; it is a matter of obedience!

What does baptism have to do with cultivating a gospel conversational culture in the local church? What, if any, is the relationship between baptisms and gospel conversations?

Introducing Gospel Conversations as a New Metric to Help Fulfill the Great Commission

Tennessee Baptist Mission Board Evangelism Specialist Steve Pearson leads a statewide evangelistic effort known as *The Reaching Tour*. The purpose of this work is the identification of what is working in evangelism today. Pearson traveled throughout the state of Tennessee meeting with churches who were "the most effective in reaching the spiritually lost."[10]

Explaining the process of selecting the most effective evangelistic churches, Pearson wrote:

> How were Reaching Tour churches discovered? We looked at the Top 10 churches in the number of baptisms from the 2015 Annual Church Profile (ACP) report. To get an accurate picture of TBC churches, we took the Top 10 from each of the four major size categories in average Sunday School attendance: (1) Churches less than 200, (2) Churches between 200-500, (3) Churches between 500-1,000, (4) Churches that average over 1000."[11]

The number of each church's baptisms played a large role in Pearson's identification of the most evangelistic churches. Indeed, baptisms remain an effective metric of measuring lost souls saved; however, could the relationship between gospel conversations and baptisms help churches become even more evangelistic?

Could the addition of a new metric help churches set and accomplish baptism goals while reaching the lost for Christ? For instance, Tennessee Baptist Churches have a statewide goal of 50,000 baptisms in 2019. One way to help accomplish that statewide goal is for each SBC church in Tennessee to set her own baptismal goal. Setting a baptismal goal is a noble cause, but how can a church see that baptismal goal become a reality?

Can gospel conversations serve as a new metric?

Research from the North American Mission Board and New Orleans Baptist Theological Seminary suggests that *one out of every ten gospel conversations result in a lost person being saved.*[12] Based on this research, Pearson and I discussed the potential of each church setting a gospel conversation goal that would result in reaching their baptismal goal.

For example, if a church sets a goal of 25 baptisms in any given year, then how many gospel conversations must be had for the attainment of that baptismal goal? Based on the research of one salvation out of every ten gospel conversations, then it would take 250 gospel conversations for this aforementioned church to see 25 salvations. See the table below for further examples.

Baptism Goal	Gospel Conversations	Baptism Attained
10	100	10
25	250	25
50	500	50
100	1000	100
50,000 Tennessee Baptist Mission Board	500,000	50,000

Since baptisms are a part of the Great Commission, then gospel conversations could potentially be a helpful metric toward fulfilling the Great Commission. Perhaps each follower of Christ and local church setting a gospel conversation goal would help in attaining baptismal goals at both the local church and state convention level. The sheer intentionality of setting a gospel conversation goal could spark a gospel conversational movement.

2. Great Commission According to Matthew

The DNA of D-Sigh-Pull-Ship

> "And Jesus came and said to them, 'All authority in heaven and on earth has been given to me. Go therefore and *make disciples of all nations,* baptizing them in the name of the Father and of the Son and of the Holy Spirit, *teaching them to*

observe all that I have commanded you. **And behold, I am with you always, to the very end of the age."' Mathew 28:18-20**

All living things have a genetic makeup known as DNA. Even cats have DNA. In fact, you can purchase DNA kits for cats. What a terrible idea! Why would anyone need to purchase a DNA kit for a cat when the known makeup of every cat is that cats don't care?

The advancements in DNA technology are impressive as DNA tests are now available for everything from solving crimes to catching dog owners who don't pick up the mess after dogs do their business. Beyond crimes and pets, when it comes to the Great Commission, what is the DNA, the genetic makeup, of discipleship?

Made disciples make disciples. If you are made into a disciple, then you are going to make disciples. Apple trees bear apples. Pear trees bear pears. Orange trees bear oranges. Disciples make disciples. If we are going to be disciples who make disciples, then four strands of the DNA of discipleship in Matthew 28:18-20 must not be ignored.

Disciple-making can't be dismissed. Jesus came to His disciples and told them about His authority. In regards to Jesus' authority, God was not playing hide and seek with the disciples. Hence, one of the themes throughout Matthew's gospel is the authority of Jesus. According to Matthew, the tax collector turned disciple of Christ, Jesus has authority over the entire universe, all nations, and every life, including you and me.

The Bible isn't a rough draft waiting on your input for the final draft. The Bible isn't one of many revised editions requiring your edits. The Bible isn't in need of an IOS update, an Apple App download, or a Netflix original. The Bible isn't going to be rewritten for you in your unfamiliar location or for your family's situation. Jesus has all authority, not some, over the universe and over you; therefore, disciple-making can't be dismissed!

Disciple-makers must be mobilized. Jesus told His disciples, in Matthew 28:19, "Go therefore and make disciples." Jesus didn't say "Google therefore" or "Gripe therefore" or "Grumble therefore." He said "Go therefore." Why is it that we are so ready to *grumble, gripe* and *Google*, yet, we are so reluctant to *go*? What did "go" ever do to us? Why does "go" get such a bad rap? Why do we tell "go" to "get gone?"

Indeed, the imperative in Matthew 28:19 is "make disciples" not "go"; however, the fact remains, if we are *going* to fulfill the Great Commission we must *go*. You can't spell *gospel* without *go*! So, why do so few *go*?

The problem is not with the *going*, but the issue is with the *leaving*. In order to *go,* one must *leave*. Leaving is hard. Leaving is uncomfortable. Leaving is costly. Leaving is unfamiliar. We will never *go* if we never *leave*. If we are ever going to experience a missional movement, there must be some movement in our mission. If we are ever going to experience a gospel conversational movement, there must be some movement toward the gospel in our conversations. What is holding you back from going and making disciples? Are you willing to leave in order to go? Disciple-makers must be mobilized!

Discipleship has to be modeled. Jesus commanded His followers "to teach them to *observe* all that I commanded you." The use of *observe* highlights the importance Jesus placed on modeling discipleship. Too many churches offer a limited model of discipleship. Lecture style discipleship, which is most often the most popular style in local churches, is ineffective. I have heard it described this way:

> Discipleship from the pulpit or any other lecture style is likened to walking into a church nursery full of babies and spraying all the babies with a single bottle of milk in hopes they are all well fed. What is the most effective way to feed babies in the nursery? Is it more effective to aimlessly spray a single bottle at all of the babies at one time? Or, is it more effective feeding each baby one bottle at a time?[13]

Churches need fewer discipleship models and more disciples modeling discipleship. In other words, if your discipleship model doesn't include disciples modeling discipleship, then a change is in order. Believers need other believers showing them how to share their testimony, study the Bible, memorize Scripture, have gospel conversations, pray, develop a quiet time with the Lord, and other spiritual disciplines.

At Red Bank Baptist Church and The Point Church, we have a discipleship pathway that includes a vehicle for modeling discipleship.

All followers of Christ are encouraged to take the next step on the discipleship pathway and bring others along. We have learned that all followers of Christ desire a path for the purpose of helping them run the race set before them.

DISCIPLESHIP PATHWAY[14]

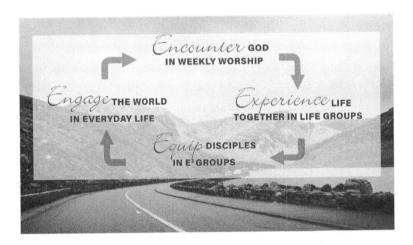

"Encounter God in Weekly Worship" takes place in our corporate worship gatherings. "Experience Life Together in Life Groups" is our small group or traditional Sunday School model. "Engage the World in Everyday Life" is engaging in everyday evangelism by having gospel conversations. "Equip Disciples in E3 Groups" is our discipleship model where discipleship is modeled.

How do we model discipleship in our discipleship model of E3 Groups? Our E3 Groups consist of 3-5 men who meet with men and 3-5 women who meet with women for the purpose of accountability, intentionality and reproducibility. The groups meet once per week for 1-11/2 hours for nine months from Labor Day to Memorial Day. From the beginning, the expectation is communicated that the goal for each person in the group is to reproduce by launching his or her own group. Some are ready to launch after going through an E3 Group once; others are not.

What happens in an E3 Group? Each person in the group journals through the Word five days a week for the purpose of sharing what God taught them each week. The E3 Group meeting begins with prayer and includes the following: telling testimony of salvation, practicing sharing the gospel with one another, divulging journal entries, discussing the Bible passages for the week, reciting memorized Scripture, reporting on gospel conversations, praying for one another, sharing struggles and temptations, and, at some point, pairing up and going out to share the gospel.

Disciples are to be multiplied. According to Matthew's gospel, Jesus' final words to His disciples were "I am with you always to the end of the age." Note, the *end of the age* is not the *end of your age* as if the making of disciples stopped with the first eleven. The gospel came to the first generation of disciples because the gospel was given for the salvation and multiplication of more generations of disciples.

Discipleship didn't start with us, and it must not end with us, but it can continue through us. All superhero blockbuster movies end the same way: the credits roll! The end of the age ends when the clouds roll back as the Rock of Ages comes in victory! Meanwhile, made disciples make disciples.

The Great Commission may be better understood as the Galilee Commission, that is, the commission given to the eleven Galileans at Galilee. Jesus is saying to all His disciples, not just the eleven, "Go back to *your* Galilee, go back to the place where I saved you, go back to the place where I began to make you disciples, then, you go and make disciples." Disciples are to be multiplied!

3. Great Commission According to Luke

Beginning in the Bible Belt

> **"Then he opened their minds to understand the Scriptures, and said to them, Thus it is written, that the Christ should suffer and on the third day rise from the dead, and that repentance and forgiveness of sins should be proclaimed in his name to all nations, *beginning from Jerusalem*. You are witnesses of these things. And behold, I am sending the**

promise of my Father upon you. But stay in the city until you are clothed with power from on high." Luke 24:45-49

Growing up in the Bible Belt exposes one to a region, most likely in the Southern United States, in which socially conservative evangelical Protestantism plays a strong role in society, culture and politics. Furthermore, Christian church attendance in the Bible Belt is generally higher than the nation's average.

Having lived in Mississippi, Louisiana, and now Tennessee means that I have lived in multiple notches in the Bible Belt's belt. The danger of being raised in the Bible Belt is reflected when people identify as Christian without having their identity in Christ, or when people are doing Christianity rather than being in Christ, or when appearance as a Christian is more important than adherence to Christ.

Dean Inserra wrote, "In the Bible Belt identifying as a Christian is a way of life, but sadly, believing the gospel and following Jesus are often not."[15] Without a doubt, the Bible Belt needs the Jesus of the Bible!

The Bible Belt needs the Jesus of the Bible. The Great Commission calls all followers of Christ to first be Jesus in your own Jerusalem, that is, the place where you live. We are to begin in our own Jerusalem. For those of us who live in the South, our Jerusalem is the Bible Belt. Even if your Jerusalem is somewhere other than the Bible Belt, you must be Jesus in your Jerusalem. The following three principles, which are applied to the Bible Belt below, are timeless, culture-less principles that can apply to any Jesus follower in any Jerusalem.

Jesus is the subject of the Bible. How can we know that Jesus is the subject of the Bible? On the road to Emmaus, Jesus, from Genesis to Malachi, preached all texts concerning Himself.

Furthermore, before Jesus commissioned His disciples, in Luke 24:44, He said, "These are my words that I spoke to you while I was still with you, that everything written about me in the Law of Moses and the Prophets and the Psalms must be fulfilled." Commenting on Luke 24:44, Leon Morris wrote: "The solemn division of Scripture into the *law of Moses and the prophets and the psalms* (the three divisions of the Hebrew Bible) indicate that there is **no part of Scripture that does not bear its witness to Jesus** (emphasis mine)."[16]

How can we be sure that Jesus is the subject of the Bible?

- **40 Different Authors** – God breathed out His Word through the writing styles of 40 different individuals and personalities.
- **1,600 Years** – Most of these authors never met, as God chose these 40 different authors over the span of 1,600 years.
- **3 Different Continents** – The Bible was written on three different continents: Asia, Africa, and Europe.
- **3 Different Languages** – The Bible was written in three different languages: Hebrew, Greek and Aramaic.
- **Hundreds of Prophecies Fulfilled by Jesus** – The odds of 48 prophecies about one person being fulfilled are 1 in 10 to the 157th power, that is 1 followed by 157 zeroes. Jesus Christ, Himself, fulfilled 300 prophecies!

What, then, can we say? When it comes to Holy Spirit-inspired authorship of the Bible, there were 40 different authors, 1,600 years, three different continents, three different languages with 100s of prophecies fulfilled, all writing about one subject: Jesus!

Can't you almost hear Jesus beginning in Genesis, moving through the Psalms and on to all the Prophets unpacking everything written about Him? Wow! Perhaps Jesus said something like this:

In Genesis, I am the Creator.
In Exodus, I am the Passover Lamb.
In Leviticus, I am the Temple.
In Numbers, I am your pillar of cloud by day and pillar of fire by night.
In Deuteronomy, I am the Coming Prophet who is greater than Moses.
In Joshua, I am the Conquering Warrior.
In Judges, I am the Savior rising up to rescue.
In Ruth, I am your Kinsman-Redeemer.
In 1 and 2 Samuel, I am the Shepherd King.
In 1 and 2 Kings, I am the Righteous Ruler.
In 1 and 2 Chronicles, I am the Restorer of the kingdom.
In Ezra, I am the Faithful Scribe.
In Nehemiah, I am the Rebuilder of the walls.

In Esther, I am your Advocate.

In Job, I am your Living Redeemer.

In the Psalms, I am the One who hears your cries.

In Proverbs, I am Wisdom personified.

In Ecclesiastes, I am the Meaning.

In Song of Solomon, I am your Lover and Bridegroom.

In Isaiah, I am the Wonderful Counselor, Mighty God, Everlasting Father, Prince of Peace, wounded for your transgressions and crushed for your iniquities.

In Jeremiah, I am the Spirit that writes God's laws on your heart.

In Lamentations, I am the Weeping Prophet.

In Ezekiel, I am the River of Life, bringing healing to the nations.

In Daniel, I am the Fourth Man in the fire.

In Hosea, I am the Forever Faithful Husband.

In Joel, I am the Restorer of all that the locusts have eaten.

In Amos, I am the Burden-Bearer.

In Obadiah, I am the Judge of all the earth.

In Jonah, I am the Prophet cast out that you can be brought in.

In Micah, I am the Everlasting Ruler born in Bethlehem.

In Nahum, I am the Avenger (*marvel at that Marvel*).

In Habakkuk, I am your Reason to rejoice.

In Zephaniah, I am the Great Reformer.

In Haggai, I am the Cleansing Fountain.

In Zechariah, I am the Pierced Son.

In Malachi, I am the Sun of Righteousness.

Jesus is also the subject of the New Testament.

In Matthew, He is the Sovereign King.

In Mark, He is the Servant.

In Luke, He is the Savior.

In John, He is the Son of God.

In Acts, He is the Risen Lord.

In Romans, He is the Justifier.

In 1 and 2 Corinthians, He is the Spirit at work in the churches.

In Galatians, He is the Righteousness imputed to us by faith.

In Ephesians, He is our Righteous Armor.

In Philippians, He is our Joy.

In Colossians, He is the Firstborn of all creation.

In 1 and 2 Thessalonians, He is descending from heaven with a shout coming to meet us in the air.

In 1 and 2 Timothy, He is the One Mediator between God and man.

In Titus, He is the Faithful Pastor.

In Philemon, He is our Liberator.

In Hebrews, He is our Great High Priest.

In James, He is faith at work.

In 1 and 2 Peter, He is our Living Cornerstone.

In 1,2 and 3 John He is the Truth, Light, Life, Love and our Assurance.

In Jude, He is God our Savior.

In Revelation, He is the King of Kings, the Lord of Lords, the Alpha and the Omega, the First and the Last, the Beginning and the End, the Living One, and the Lamb slain before the foundation of the world. The Bible has always and only ever been about Jesus![17]

Jesus is the subject of the Bible and should be the subject of our conversations. Jesus, who is the subject of the Bible, has made us subject to gospel conversations about Him. Why is it important that Jesus is the subject of the Bible and should be the subject of our conversations?

Jesus appeared to His disciples in His resurrected state, but they didn't recognize Him until He opened their minds to the Scriptures. Is it any wonder that faith comes from hearing the Word of Christ, not seeing the wounds of Christ? Praise God that faith comes from hearing Jesus' Word and not seeing Jesus' wounds as only the first-century disciples saw Jesus' wounds. The fact that faith comes from hearing and not seeing opens the door for all who lived before Jesus and after Jesus to hear and be saved!

Jesus is the Savior in the Bible Belt. According to Luke 24:46-47, the gospel message is "that the Christ should suffer and on the third day rise from the dead, and that repentance and forgiveness of sins should be proclaimed in his name to all nations, beginning from Jerusalem." Yes, Jesus is the Savior of the whole world, including the Bible Belt.

Jerusalem is where we must start proclaiming the gospel of Jesus calling people to repent.

We have way too many excuses for not sharing our faith in our own Jerusalem. Some common excuses include:

○ **I don't know any lost people.** Have you looked in the mirror? Are you saved? Start with yourself.

○ **I am afraid I might push my friends away.** One evangelist said, "So, you're afraid sharing Jesus will push unbelievers away? They're already away!"[18]

○ **I am not allowed to share the gospel at work or school.** Sure, you may not be able to lead a devotional or prayer meeting at work or school; however, if a person asks you about your faith, then you can tell them about Jesus.

○ **I am afraid I don't know enough.** As a believer, you need to be afraid not because you don't know enough, but because you know plenty and are unwilling to share. If you know enough of the gospel to be saved, then you know enough of the gospel to share. Charles Spurgeon said, "A man says to me, 'Can you explain the seven trumpets of the Revelation?' No, but I can blow one in your ear, and warn you to escape from the wrath to come."[19]

○ **Can't I just build a relationship with my friend and let him or her see Jesus in me, rather than tell them about Jesus?** All believers should always live a life that points to Jesus. What we must remember is that faith doesn't come from seeing the wounds of life, but hearing the Word of Christ. When people see us living for Jesus, often times, we earn the right to share Jesus, but we must share. If we simply befriend people without sharing the gospel, then we are merely befriending them to Hell.

Jesus is sovereign over the Bible Belt and beyond. In Luke 24:49, Jesus said, "And behold, I am sending the promise of my Father upon you. But stay in the city until you are clothed with power from on high." Did Jesus fulfill this promise? Did Jesus send the promised Holy Spirit?

How do we know if we can trust the sovereignty of Jesus? The Apostle Luke is the author the Holy Spirit inspired to pen the Gospel of Luke. Here, at the end of Luke, we know that God isn't finished with Luke.

Do you know how we know that at the end of the Gospel of Luke God wasn't finished with Luke? Luke wrote another book. Luke wrote the book of Acts. Jesus was sovereign over Luke and all that He had for him. In the same way, Jesus is sovereign over you and every single gospel conversation He has planned for you as you make the Great Commission great again. From the Bible Belt and beyond, Jesus is the subject of the Bible, the Savior of the world, and the Sovereign over all!

4. Great Commission According to John

You Are Sent

"Jesus said to them again, 'Peace be with you. As the Father has sent me, even so I am sending you.' And when he had said this, he breathed on them and said to them, 'Receive the Holy Spirit. If you forgive the sins of any, they are forgiven them; if you withhold forgiveness from any, it is withheld.'" John 20:21-23

The 396 young men began that day as students in caps and gowns, ready to graduate from Morehouse College—full of hope, but burdened in most cases with the student loan debts that financed their education. Then, their commencement speaker went off-script with an extraordinary pledge. The newly minted 2019 graduating class of the historically black Morehouse College in Atlanta would be sent out into the world student debt-free; they would go forth into the world with all student loans paid in full.

Robert F. Smith, the billionaire investor, during his commencement speech, told the crowd that he and his family would pay off the entire graduating class's forty-million dollar student loan debt. The whole graduating class would be free to go forth into the world and begin their next chapter without any student loan payments.[20]

As you can imagine, the graduates were elated and liberated by, perhaps, the greatest commencement speech ever. What a way to send out graduates, debt-free! What a novel idea! You do realize that as followers of Jesus, He has sent us out, not only sin debt-free but also supplied for every need. In Jesus' Great Commissioning speech, not the greatest commencement speech, let's see how Jesus sends us!

Jesus sends us. First of all, we must know that as followers of Jesus, we are not sent out by a college, seminary, denomination, convention, church or board; we are sent out by Jesus. The good news is that Jesus sends us fully forgiven and fully equipped for every good work. In John's account of the Great Commission, there are no less than five needs Jesus meets as He sends us.

Jesus speaks to His saints. John's Great Commission text begins with the words "Jesus said to them again." Jesus didn't speak about them, at them, or above them; He spoke *to* them. Jesus spoke to people, not about people, not at people, and not above people. Why are we so quick to speak about people, at people and even above people, rather than speaking to people?

The fact that Jesus said to them *again* is both comforting and convicting. Jesus' use of the word *again* is comforting in that there is never a time when He is not speaking. At the same time, His use of the word *again* is convicting in that there is never a time when He is not speaking. In our times of struggle or thriving, disobedience or obedience, faith or lack of faith, plenty or little, and even faithfulness or unfaithfulness, Jesus is always speaking.

Why is Jesus speaking again and again? We need to hear Him again and again! As Jesus sends us, He continues speaking to us!

Jesus comforts Christians. With a simple but powerful statement, "Peace be with you," Jesus comforts Christians. Every follower of Christ should be overjoyed that Jesus didn't say, "Drama be with you" or "Justice be with you" or "Judgment be with you" or "War be with you." Jesus said "Peace be with you!" Peace is not the absence of something, but the presence of someone; that someone is Jesus.

To whom was Jesus speaking when He offered peace? Contextually, Jesus was speaking to His disciples as they were terrified and locked in a room in fear of the Jews. Holistically, Jesus was including all who will come to Him alone, through faith alone, by grace alone. The encouraging aspect of Jesus' "Peace be with you" to His disciples in John

20 is that Jesus was offering them peace right then and there in their current state of fear.

Avoid falling for Satan's lie that you must clean yourself up before Jesus will give you peace. Jesus offers His peace to you right now in all of your brokenness, pain, doubt, shame, deceit, unforgiveness, hopelessness, fear, disappointments, anger and bitterness. Jesus offers His peace to *you*, not an updated version of you, not a "let me get myself cleaned up" you, not a "try harder you," not a "rub some dirt on it" you, not a "shake it off" you, not a "pull up your bootstraps" you, not a "where you will be in the future" you, but a "where you are right now" you.

As a follower of Christ, where do you find comfort?

- ○ **Comfort zone** – Your comfort zone may provide you with familiarity and routine, but that is not comfort. Don't mistake routine and what is familiar as comfort.
- ○ **Comfort in our country** – Our country offers no comfort. We live in a nation that says a man can't talk about abortion since he doesn't have a uterus. At the same time, that same nation says that a man can be a woman even if he doesn't have a uterus. That's chaos, not comfort!
- ○ **Comfort in being comfortable** – Also, there is no comfort in what is comfortable, such as adventure, business, creativity, brown truck deliveries (especially at my house), education, finances, vacations, staycations, retirement or career.

The Only place we find comfort and peace is in the person of Jesus. Jesus didn't come to give us a piece of His mind or peace of mind. He came to give us peace. Jesus has more comfort than we have discomfort, more forgiveness than we have unforgiveness, more peace than we have problems, more strength than we have weakness, more grace than we have sin, and more love than we have hate. Jesus comforts Christians.

Jesus deploys His disciples. Jesus said to His disciples "As the Father has sent me, I am sending you." I used to be a cool dad, but my coolness has cooled off and grown cold. Two of my daily dad duties are as follows: (1) turn off the lights in the house, and (2) turn up the radio in the car. No longer am I cool, but God the Father remains the coolest.

How cool it is that God the Father allows us to be sent out by Jesus as Jesus was sent out by Him!

Don't forget how Jesus was sent. Jesus didn't wait on us to come to Him; He came to us. Jesus took the initiative and met us right where we were. He still meets people right where they are. Jesus came to love the unlovable, reach the unreachable, touch the untouchable, and forgive the unforgivable. How can we do any less? The Son of God is sending out the children of God to tell the world about the One Mediator between man and God. Jesus deploys His disciples.

Jesus empowers evangelicals. The Bible says that Jesus "breathed on them and said to them, Receive the Holy Spirit." Did the Holy Spirit come at the moment when Jesus was commissioning His disciples? No. How do we know this was not the time of the coming of the Holy Spirit?

○ **Thomas was absent** – Thomas, one of the disciples, was absent at this time. The Promised Holy Spirit would not come while any of the eleven were absent. The Holy Spirit was promised to all the disciples, not some. There is no such thing as a follower of Jesus who doesn't have the Holy Spirit.

○ **Jesus was still present** – Jesus told His disciples that unless He leaves them, then the Holy Spirit will not come. Therefore, Jesus couldn't be present in the flesh when the promised Holy Spirit arrived.

So, what is meant by Jesus breathing on them and saying "Receive the Holy Spirit?" Just as Jesus is the only way to the Father, He is also the only way anyone will ever receive the Holy Spirit. When a person puts their faith alone, by grace alone, in Christ alone, then he or she is sealed with the promised Holy Spirit. Jesus has the power to not only save us but send us. Jesus empowers evangelicals.

Jesus forgives His followers. Jesus closed this Great Commission text speaking about forgiveness. He said *If you forgive the sins of any, they are forgiven them; if you withhold forgiveness from any, it is withheld.* What is Jesus teaching exactly?

When a follower of Christ shares the gospel, one of two things happen: (1) a person believes, repents and is forgiven, or (2) a person does not believe and remains unforgiven. The only determining factor between forgiveness and unforgiveness is belief and repentance or disbelief and unrepentance toward the gospel of Jesus.

For Christ-followers, the gospel also offers power to restore and reconcile relationships through forgiveness. Perhaps these nine questions can help you discern if you are harboring unforgiveness in your heart:

- ○ **Has someone deeply hurt your or your family?**
- ○ **Do you still get angry or anxious when you think about the person who hurt you?**
- ○ **If that person is dead, are you justifying your continued anger?**
- ○ **Do you quietly hope that person hurts like you?**
- ○ **Would you help that person if he/she needed it?**
- ○ **Are you able to pray for that person?**
- ○ **If God blessed them, would you be frustrated?**
- ○ **Will you avoid that person the next time you see him or her?**

If you need to forgive someone, then pause right now and ask the Holy Spirit to help you forgive. Jesus empowers you to do so. Remember, not only can the unforgiven be forgiven, but the forgiven must forgive.

5. Great Commission According to Luke in Acts

We Are Witnesses

> **"But you will receive power when the Holy Spirit comes upon you, and you will be my witnesses in Jerusalem and in all Judea and Samaria, and to the end of the earth." Acts 1:8**

As the story goes, a young man applied for a job as an usher at a concert hall. The manager asked him, "What would you do in case a fire breaks out?" The young man answered, "Don't worry about me. I'd get out okay."[21] What about all the other patrons in the concert hall? How will they escape?

We must guard against the same WEology and MEology as this

young usher: "Don't worry about ME or us. WE know we will escape the fires of hell." What about everyone else? Jesus didn't leave this planet without a plan to send you and me for the purpose of reaching the lost.

Jesus ascent means we are sent. After Jesus' death, burial, resurrection, appearing to, and commissioning of His disciples, He ascended back to the Father. What is meant by Jesus' ascent? The ascent of the Lord Jesus back to heaven meant and still means only one thing for Christ-followers: we are sent! There is no question about the fact that we are sent. How are we sent? That is the question. Jesus offered four characteristics explaining the manner in which He sends us out.

We are sent as known witnesses. In Jesus' statement, "But you will receive power," the *you* is plural, not singular. The plural form of *you* simply means that Jesus is including all of His disciples in His commissioning. Whether you are young and energetic like an Avenger evangelist, or you at an age where you are restless of business-as-usual Baptists, cookie-cutter Christianity, dull and dead doctrine or rude religion, or even if you are at the age when it is time for a dental appointment you send out your teeth, the Great Commission is for you.

Jesus knows who you are, where you are and what you are facing; yet, He still sends you out as His witness. Just like Jesus' first disciples, too many of us, however, want to be in the know and know-it-alls. Being a know-it-all has one problem: the one thing know-it-alls don't know is they are known-by-all as being a know-it-all. Jesus has not called us to be in the know or to be know-it-alls; He has called us as known witnesses.

We are sent as now witnesses. Jesus told His disciples that they would receive power only when the Holy Spirit came upon them. At Pentecost, the Holy Spirit came and empowered Jesus' disciples. After Pentecost, every time a person places his or her faith alone, by grace alone, in Christ alone, at that moment he or she receives the Holy Spirit.

In our present age, baptism by Christ through the Holy Spirit takes place at the moment a person comes to saving faith in Christ. Furthermore, each follower of Christ gets all the Holy Spirit at conversion. The question for believers is not: "How much of the Holy Spirit do you have?" The question for believers is: "How much of you does the Holy Spirit have?" In other words, upon salvation, you become a now witness right then and there.

Have you ever checked out of a grocery store or retail store and received a printed receipt showcasing the amount of money you saved while shopping? This is a fundamental problem. If you are shopping, then you are not saving. If you are saving, then you are not shopping. Rather than printing "You saved" on the receipt, the business should print a more accurate description such as "You did not spend."

The only receipt that can ever accurately claim true savings is the resurrection of Jesus. The resurrection of Jesus is the receipt guaranteeing the salvation of any who trust in Him. If you have placed your trust in Jesus, then you are, right now, a now witness.

We are sent as new witnesses. "You will be my witnesses" is the commissioning that Jesus extends to all who follow Him. From the old covenant to the birth of the church, Jesus makes all things new. As followers of Jesus, we are bought at a price. Is Jesus getting what He paid for? We are no longer our own. We belong to Jesus. We should be excited about Jesus making all things new, including us!

Have you ever noticed the stoic facial expressions found on photographs from years gone by? Let it not be said of disciples of Jesus that the lack of joy in our life matches these old stoic photographs.

Charles Spurgeon once said, "When you speak of heaven, let your face light up. When you speak of hell, well then, your everyday face will do."[22]

David Hume, a well-known Scottish skeptic from the 18th Century, who was a Deist and didn't believe in the gospel of Jesus, traveled twenty miles to hear George Whitefield preach. About 5:00 a.m. one morning, he was walking down the street in London. As he came around the corner, another man saw him and said,

"Why, aren't you David Hume?"

Hume replied, "Yes."

The man asked Hume, "Where are you going so early in the morning?"

Hume answered, "I am going to hear George Whitfield preach."

"I didn't think you believed the gospel," said the man.

"I don't," replied Hume, "but he does!"[23]

Do people believe that you believe the gospel? Can people tell that you have been made new by Christ and are new in Christ? Does the aroma of your life have that new car smell or that old bus seat smell?

We are sent as a network of witnesses. The Great Commission is to begin in Jerusalem, your Jerusalem and mine, and be fulfilled to the end of the earth. The good news is that we are not alone in carrying the good news of Jesus to our neighbors and the nations.

Have you ever noticed that the book of Acts is the only unfinished book of the Bible? In Acts 28:28, the book of Acts ends with "Therefore let it be known to you that this salvation of God has been sent to the Gentiles; they will listen." Apparently, since they will listen, there is no deficiency in the harvest, but the laborers are lacking. Are you praying for laborers? Are you laboring in the work of the gospel? If not, why not?

Acts 29 Network, a network of churches and church planters, exists because the work of church planting is unfinished. The work of redemption is finished, but the work of telling every language, tribe, nation and people that the work of redemption is finished remains unfinished.

Will you make the unfinished business of telling people about Christ's finished work your business?

The Churches Conservation Trust is a UK charity whose purpose is to protect historic churches at risk in England. The collection of churches conserved by the trust is the third largest collection of heritage buildings in the UK.[24] How sad it is that these churches were once vibrant places of worship and viable centers of Great Commission work.

Too many churches in the UK and the US are on life support. We need less good conservational churches and gossip controversial churches and more gospel conversational churches. Jesus is building His church through the empowerment of gospel conversing people, not the endorsement of conserving buildings.

REFLECTION QUESTIONS

○ What would happen if local churches would decide to live out the imperatives found in these five Great Commissions?

○ What would your church need to change in order to fulfill these Great Commission imperatives?

○ What would it take for you and your church to do whatever it takes to fulfill the Great Commission?

○ In what ways do the five Great Commissions help to cultivate a gospel conversational culture in local churches?

CHAPTER II

Missing the Mode of Everyday Evangelism

"Just 1% of believers claim to have the gift of evangelism."[25] – Ed Stetzer

My GPS Went Missing

My name is Sam, and I am digitally and technologically inept. So, you can imagine what a moment of satisfaction it was upon successfully downloading the app, placing my order, and tracking the delivery of that chicken tortilla soup. By completing the order, especially before my wife Tonya was able to order pizza for our girls, I felt a real sense of accomplishment. Little did I know that it would soon be, *no soup for me!*

I placed the order with one of those food delivery service companies that delivers food for restaurants that don't deliver. I ordered the food on the delivery service app at 4:44 p.m. The app then communicated that the food would be delivered in 36 minutes by a driver named Charles. Well, the process of ordering food on the delivery app seemed simple enough, right? Wrong!

One hour, that's right, sixty minutes after placing the order, the app reported that my food would now be delivered between 86 to 96 minutes. The first driver, Charles, vanished. The new driver was Angela. She was on her way to the restaurant to pick-up the food. One hour and thirty-one minutes after placing the order, the app reported that Angela finally arrived at the restaurant and the food would be delivered in twenty-two minutes.

Thirty minutes later or two hours and one minute after placing the order, for those of you who are counting, Angela called my cell phone and said: "My GPS went out and I have no way to deliver your food."

What did we ever do before British speaking GPS voices? How did anything get delivered before GPS? Did people actually read maps? Yes, some even printed maps off MapQuest.

Meanwhile, Angela is trying to describe her whereabouts; however, she is still aimlessly driving. I suggest that she stop at a nearby business. She agreed. At this point, I knew there was only one thing left to do: go meet her and deliver my food myself.

Two hours and fifteen minutes after ordering, I pull up next to Angela and her whole family is in the car as they are enjoying a fast food meal. She hands me my bag of soup, which smells like a chimney of cigarette smoke, and says, "This is the first time my GPS has gone out." Tonya and the girls had already eaten pizza, cleaned up the kitchen and were watching a movie by the time my soup and I arrived.

The kicker of this true story is that I ended up driving a farther distance to meet the delivery driver than had I just driven to the restaurant. Did I mention this was my first time using this type of delivery service? Well, actually, I have used this service twice, at the same time, both my first and last!

Different modes of restaurant and grocery food distribution exist: (1) dine-in, (2) order-in and takeout, (3) call-in and takeout, (4) online order and takeout, (5) curbside, and (6) multiple options for delivery, including, apparently, deliver your food to yourself.

For the Greer family, there will be at least one mode of food distribution missing from future options: food delivery services. I know—what a terrible attitude. Perhaps over time we will be open to the idea, perhaps not.

Far too many followers of Christ are missing out on the blessing of delivering the gospel of Jesus because they are suffering from the missing mode of *everyday evangelism*. In fact, only 1% of believers claim to have the gift of evangelism.[26] If 99% of believers, who don't claim to have the gift of evangelism, believe that evangelism is a gift, then that same 99% may never share their faith.

Evangelism is not a gift; it's a work in which every believer must engage. Hence, the missing mode of everyday evangelism must be found by all believers!

What is evangelism? For effective evangelism to occur, there must be an announcer of the good news of Jesus announcing the good news of Jesus. Several definitions of evangelism may be helpful in understanding that all believers are called to evangelize.

Consider the following definitions given by different evangelistic enthusiasts:

Paul McCauley and David Williamson defined evangelism as "telling sinners the gospel so that they may be saved."[27]

Matt Queen offered a more extensive definition of evangelism as he wrote, "Evangelism is that Spirit-empowered activity in which disciples of Jesus Christ give an intentional, verbal, and complete witness to the life, death, burial, and resurrection of Jesus Christ, calling unbelievers to become disciples of Jesus Christ by repenting of their sins and placing their faith in Jesus Christ alone."[28]

Laura Yang added that evangelism is "the sharing of the good news of Jesus Christ," which is "something God wants us to do every day."[29]

John Mark Terry wrote that "evangelism is presenting Jesus Christ in the power of the Holy Spirit so that people will become his disciples."[30]

How do we know that the mode of everyday evangelism is missing?

Queen wrote: "What if every member of your church made evangelism a regular practice in his or her daily routine? Imagine the impact this would have on your church and your community! Sadly, though, what should be a natural part of the Christian life is often neglected or passed off to 'the experts.'"[31]

Laura Yang asked, "Do you struggle with sharing your Christian faith? You are not alone! Most Christians do. In fact, only two percent of church members invite an unchurched person to church. Ninety-eight percent of churchgoers never extend an invitation in a given year."[32]

McCauley and Williamson argued, "Evangelism, so the argument goes, is the work of the evangelist, a man gifted by God for that work. It seems pointless to show evangelists how to evangelise—they already know. It's a waste of time teaching other Christians to evangelise—it's not their job. While this is the thinking of many, it is not the teaching of the New Testament."[33]

How do we find the missing mode of everyday evangelism? First, we must consider the modes of evangelism found in the early church. Second, we must consider the modes of evangelism found in the local church today. Third, we must consider the main mode of evangelism found in the Gospels. Fourth, we must find the missing mode of everyday evangelism today.

1. Modes of evangelism found in the early church

"And day by day, attending the temple together and breaking bread in their homes, they received their food with glad and generous hearts, praising God and having favor with all the people. And the Lord added to their number day by day those who were being saved." Acts 2:46-47

How is it that the Lord added to the early church each day those who were being saved? People were saved in the early church the same way people are saved today. Faith in Christ comes from hearing the Word of Christ. Obviously, then, the early church heard the gospel, shared the gospel, preached the gospel, and had gospel conversations. Can we glean any insight into the different modes of evangelism in the early church?

Preaching and teaching the gospel in the temple. The early church attended the temple together as they devoted themselves to the apostles' teaching. When Jesus' parents forgot about him and left him at the temple (parents, I know you would never), Jesus was found listening to the teachers and asking questions. Peter and John, on the way to the temple at the hour of prayer, healed a man born lame in the name of Jesus the Christ. Whether in the temple in Jerusalem or a Starbucks in your Jerusalem, the gospel can't be stopped!

Sharing the gospel from home to home. What better place to share the gospel than in a home! From house to house, the early church broke bread together and worshiped together. Like the early church, we would do well to take advantage of building relationships with friends and neighbors in our home.

Everyday conversations to gospel conversations. The Lord granted the early church favor as they engaged people in everyday life. Evangelistic fervor, coupled with everyday favor with everyone, resulted in a gospel conversational movement in the early church.

Jesus is the same today as He was yesterday. Jesus' commission is the same today as it was yesterday. Jesus' gospel is the same today as it was yesterday. What has changed? Could it be that Jesus' church has changed from being on fire for the gospel to watering down the gospel and from being sold out for the gospel to selling out the gospel?

While studying the different modes of evangelism in the early church, Michael Green observed, "Indeed, for more than 150 years they (the early church) possessed no church buildings, and there was the greatest variety in the type and content of Christian evangelistic preaching."[34] The different modes of evangelism in the early church recorded by Green are as follows:

- ○ **Synagogue Preaching** – The synagogue was the place where the Torah was read, and the Jews gathered weekly. What an opportunity the synagogue provided for Jesus, His disciples and other Christ-followers to preach the gospel to the Jews and some God-fearing Gentiles. Green wrote, "The synagogue provided the seedbed for evangelism among the Jews."[35]
- ○ **Open-Air Preaching** – Jesus often preached in impromptu open-air meetings. The Gospels and Acts give multiple examples of open-air preaching.
- ○ **Telling of Personal Testimonies** – The whole of the New Testament is peppered with personal testimony after personal testimony of faith in Christ. Many, if not all, of the New Testament writers, added personal testimony to the message they received from the Holy Spirit.
- ○ **Invasion of Home Evangelism** – Household evangelism was key in the early church. Homes provided a place where conversations flourished. As it is today, preaching was more of an epilogue in the 1st Century, while home evangelism was more of a dialogue.

- ○ **Personal Encounters** – Personal evangelism, whereby one individual shares his or her faith with another, was just as important as any other mode of evangelism in the early church. The gospel comes to each person for the purpose of being passed on to the next person.
- ○ **Visiting** – Some believe that cold-call evangelism is dead, but that is baloney with a capital "B!" Even if cold-call evangelism is dead today, it was alive and well in the times of the early church. Jesus cold-called Zacchaeus as He visited him in his house.
- ○ **Literary Evangelism** – State of the art technology in the times of the early church was letter writing. Letter writing was the social media of the day in the ancient days. In fact, the first four books of the New Testament, the Gospels, are evidence that authors took advantage of writing to share the gospel.[36]

2. Modes of evangelism found in the local church today

"A church centered on the gospel of Jesus Christ will be turned inside out because the gospel rightly grasped compels a church to join God's mission in the world."[37] – Jared C. Wilson

Over the past several years, the city of Chattanooga, TN, has consistently ranked as one of the, if not the, most Bible-minded city in America.[38] Even still, 50% of Chattanoogans, which is most likely a conservative percentage, remain unchurched. In Chattanooga and beyond, local churches must localize evangelism. What are the modes of evangelism that are still working in the local church today? Most local church evangelistic strategies can be included in one of the following three modes of evangelism.

Come and see. Most evangelical, gospel-preaching churches utilize the "come and see" or "you come to us" mode of evangelism. Weekly gatherings of like-minded followers of Christ in corporate worship and other evangelistic events present opportunities for the presence of non-members and non-believers. Another description of this mode of evangelism is "Body-Life Witness" which is described as evangelism through the witness "of a body of believers."[39] Hopefully, when people "come and see" they also "come and hear" the gospel of Jesus preached and taught.

Go and tell. Some evangelical, gospel-preaching churches utilize the "go and tell" mode of evangelism. Whether it be local, national or international mission trips, back-yard Bible clubs, VBS in neighborhoods, sports camps, weekly evangelistic visitations, community workdays or any other ministry outreach, followers of Christ go into communities and tell people about Jesus. "Ministry Witness," which is the witness of a Christ-follower "who had contact with a person primarily through a ministry outreach," is another term which captures the essence of the "go and tell" mode.[40]

Jared C. Wilson commented on the transition from a "come and see" to a "go and tell" church mentality. He wrote, "Transitioning from an attractional mindset to a missional mindset means understanding that the church isn't simply 'people in place' (come and see) but also 'people in places' (go and tell). It prioritizes the missional strategy of 'go and tell' over 'come and see.'"[41]

Tell as you go. Few evangelical, gospel-preaching churches utilize the "tell and go" mode of evangelism. The participle "Go" in Matthew's account of the Great Commission can be understood as "as you are going." As believers are going about everyday life, we must be turning everyday conversations into gospel conversations. Another way to understand the "tell and go" mode is by sharing Christ with those with whom you already have a relationship. Other terms for the "tell and go" mode include gospel conversations, everyday evangelism, soul-winning, witnessing, relational evangelism, or personal evangelism.

3. Main mode of evangelism found in the Gospels

"Follow me, and I will make you fishers of men." Matthew 4:19

"Go therefore and make disciples of all nations…." Matthew 28:19

In Matthew 4:18, when Jesus called Peter and Andrew, they were "casting a net into the sea." Jesus could have called these fishermen at any time, but He called them at a very specific time for a very significant reason. The disciples *casting* the net has a direct correlation to personal evangelism. Jesus spoke at just the right time for the disciples to understand that their responsibility and ours is to *cast* for people, not *catch* people.

Jesus has called us to be *casters*, not *catchers*. Too many pastors and churches, however, are asking the wrong questions.

Two questions often asked of and by pastors are as follows:

○ *"How many is your church running?"*
○ *"How many is your church catching?"*

Two better questions pastors and churches should be asking:

○ *"How many in your church are fishing?"*
○ *"How many in your church are teaching others to fish?"*

Being "fishers of men" who make "fishers of men" means Jesus will not ask us how many we caught, but He will ask us how many we *taught*.

Tonya and I are the blessed parents of two girls. Tonya doesn't like to fish, neither does our oldest daughter Braydee. Belle, our youngest, loves to fish. Though allergic to fish, I love teaching her how to fish. Teaching Belle how to cast her bait-casting reel is one of the joys of being her dad. Watching her make her first cast was just as rewarding as seeing her catch her first bass. Fishing is fun, but teaching Belle how to fish is rewarding.

What, then, is the main mode of evangelism in the Gospels? The main mode of evangelism in the Gospels is personal evangelism, that is, having gospel conversations. We must begin to take personal evangelism personally. Who are you teaching to fish for people? Though you may be allergic to sharing your faith, God expects you to not only share your faith, but also to teach others to share their faith. What is keeping you from following Jesus and fishing for people?

How, then, must we understand the main mode of evangelism in the Gospels? Jesus' first and last words to His disciples were similar. Matthew 4:19 records Jesus' first words to His disciples as He called them, "I will make you fishers of men." Matthew 28:19 records Jesus' last words to His disciples as He commissioned them: "Go therefore and make disciples of all nations." Jesus called these fishermen to be made into "fishers of men." Then, He commissioned them to go make disciples. How are this call and commission different?

A helpful exercise in discerning the difference between Jesus' call to His disciples and commission of His disciples is to examine the grammatical mood of these two statements. In grammar, moods are forms of the verb that express how the action or event is presented by the speaker.

Four different moods are found in Greek grammar: indicative, imperative, subjunctive, and operative. These four grammatical moods are not referring to moods we may have before, during, or after Starbucks:

○ **The indicative mood** presents the action or event as an objective fact. For example, "The door is opened."
○ **The imperative mood** expresses a command, such as "Shut the door!"
○ **The subjunctive mood** describes a probable situation; for example, "The door may be opened."
○ **The operative mood** identifies an obtainable wish as indicated by "I wish the door was opened."[42]

Jesus' call to His disciples, "I will make you fishers of men," was in the indicative mood, which is an objective fact. On the contrary, Jesus' commission of His disciples, "make disciples," was in the imperative mood, which is a command.

In the Bible, indicatives tell us what has been or will be done, while imperatives tell us what we must do. Indicative moods are descriptive as they describe an action. Imperative moods are prescriptive as they prescribe an action. Indicatives are stated facts, and imperatives are commands.

Confusion in interpretation arises when we mistake indicatives for imperatives and imperatives for indicatives. Jesus' commissioning of the disciples found in Matthew 28 is not a description of a one-time, isolated event. Rather, the Great Commission is a prescribed commission for every follower of Jesus in any and all generations.

Although we aren't always present in fulfilling the Great

Commission, the good news is that Jesus is never absent from it. Every follower of Christ, then, must engage in the main mode of evangelism found in the Gospels. We must find the missing mode of *everyday evangelism* every day!

4. Finding the missing mode of *everyday evangelism* every day

"There is nothing more freeing than abandoning your own mission and joining the everyday mission of God."[43] – Dustin Willis and Aaron Coe

The Magic Kingdom was so magical that my four-year-old, Belle, inadvertently left her stuffed companion, B, in the park. After an exhausting day in the park, as we were walking through the hotel lobby on the way to our room, Belle began to wail.

"B! Where's B?" B was lost. Immediately, I became intimately acquainted with Disney World's Lost and Found department. Every hour, I called them to see if B had been dropped off. About midnight, they told me that a stuffed bear may have been found.

Early the next morning, I caught a bus from the hotel to lost and found. The pleasant lady driving the bus boasted that Disney World had over a 90% recovery rate of lost items. A glimmer of hope was in the cool January air.

Upon arriving at lost and found, I noticed I was one of about three dads. The lost and found office had the feel of a shameful place where irresponsible parents were held accountable.

One of the dads looked at me and said, "What are you in for?" Sitting behind the lost and found desk was a uniformed security guard. "Next!"

One of the dads in front of me shimmied up to the desk. The security guard interrogated him with a parade of questions. Then, it was my turn to face the intimidating guard.

After a grueling cross-examination, the guard disappeared into the next room and re-appeared with B in tow. We were on the positive side of the 90% recovery rate. I have never been so excited to see a stuffed bear and couldn't wait for Belle and B to be reunited.

In John 14:6, Jesus said, "I am the way, and the truth, and the life. No man comes to the Father except through me." The exclusivity of Christ is foundational truth.

No one, 0%, will be gathered to the Father unless they come through the Son. It is also true that everyone, 100%, will be gathered to the Father if they come through the Son.

Disney World may have a 90% recovery rate of lost items, but the good news is that 100% of the lost who come to Jesus will be found. Goodness, the good news is so good as it is a reminder of God's goodness!

Yet, the sad news is so sad. What is the sad news? If 99% of believers believe that evangelism is a gift and only 1% of believers claim to have that gift, then the sad news is that 100% of the lost ever hearing the gospel rests upon 1% of the saved. Do you really believe that is God's plan?

We live in a world of everyday pain, suffering, disappointment, violence, abuse, lust, loneliness, bitterness, anger, envy, and all kinds of other brokenness. Indeed, we are broken people surrounded by broken people in an everyday broken world. Moreover, God remains steadfast in not desiring anyone remain in brokenness.

Believers, in all of our brokenness, God didn't throw us away, try to repair us, or simply make us better. In Christ, God made us new! Every day that we wake up, the gospel is making us new!

Since the gospel is making us new every day, then shouldn't we be making the gospel known every day? Every day there is someone who is one text away, one smile away, one street away, one cubicle away, or some other encounter away who needs to hear how Jesus broke your brokenness!

REFLECTION QUESTIONS

○ What would you include in your personal definition of evangelism? Write it out.
○ What can be learned from the modes of evangelism in the early church?

○ Of the three modes of evangelism, which one does your church do well?

○ In which mode of evangelism does your church need improvement?

○ How do you see your role in personal evangelism?

CHAPTER III

Ignoring Your Oikos
is not Okay

"95% of all believers give credit to someone in their oikos for leading them to Jesus."[44] – Tom Mercer

Team Tonya

When Tonya and I were standing on the beach in Maui, Hawaii, reciting our wedding vows, *in sickness and in health*, we never dreamed of any sickness. At twenty-seven and twenty-four years old, we were only thinking about health. Then, sixteen years later, *that day* came. Oh, how I will never forget *that day*.

That day was the day we walked into the doctor's office. Like any other doctor's office on any day of the week, the waiting room was full of patients waiting to see the doctor. When we walked into the office, I was checking out what magazine might entertain for the next couple of hours.

As soon as the nurse saw us, she went back to get the doctor, and something happened that I have never experienced before and hope I never will again. The doctor walked out into the waiting room straight toward us and said, "Y'all come with me."

We followed the doctor back to the second waiting room. You do know about the second waiting room, right? The waiting room behind the waiting room where you are normally left waiting again. Well, we didn't even have to wait in the second waiting room. The doctor walked in, closed the door, and said: "Tonya, it's cancer." I didn't hear anything else. I was stunned.

I used to be the person who would moan, groan and complain about waiting in a doctor's office waiting room. But, now, I am the person who can't wait to wait in the doctor's waiting room, because the alternative is devastating.

In April of 2017, Tonya was diagnosed with a rare form of cancer known as appendiceal and peritoneal carcinoma. In August of that same year, she underwent a long and intrusive Hyperthermic Intraperitoneal Chemotherapy (HIPEC) surgery. Part of the surgery included bathing Tonya's intestines in heated chemo. Her surgery was successful, but recovery was brutal as more surgeries were required. Ultimately, God healed Tonya. She is 1½ years' cancer-free, and we are blessed.

I have heard it said, "I don't see how anybody makes it through life's trouble without Jesus." I amen that twice: Amen! Amen! Yet, I would also say, "I don't see how anybody makes it through life's trouble without Jesus' church."

Team Tonya became the slogan for Tonya's cancer battle, and we are appreciative for all who joined the team. Though forever thankful, we will never be able to thank our church family at Red Bank Baptist Church enough for all the prayers, support, food (especially the food), cards, acts of service, and so much more. So many churches from Chattanooga and beyond prayed for Tonya and supported us in ways we could never think or imagine.

Again, let me reiterate, I don't see how anyone makes it through life's trouble without a personal relationship with Jesus *and* without being connected to His church. Ignoring Jesus is not okay. Ignoring Jesus' church is not okay. Ignoring *your* oikos, given to you by Jesus, is not okay. How can we avoid ignoring our oikos? The following four guardrails will help us avoid ignoring our oikos.

Identify your oikos

"Oikos is not a program. It's not an event. It's not an emphasis. It's actually like a new pair of glasses through which we can see the world as Jesus did."[45] Mercer.

What is *oikos*? "Oikos" is a Greek word transliterated as "house, household, family, and family household."[46] Tom Mercer defined *oikos* as an "extended household" and offered the following four characteristics of any given *oikos*:

- ○ **Evangelistic environment** – Oikos is the most natural and common environment for evangelism to occur.
- ○ **8 to 15** – Oikos is a group of eight to fifteen people with whom you share life most closely, your sphere of greatest influence.
- ○ **Gospel conversations** – Your oikos is made up of the people for whom God wants to prepare you to become an ideal instrument of His grace through gospel conversations.
- ○ **Gospel conversions** – Any and every oikos is a microcosm of the world at large, for whom God sent His Son—that all who place their faith in Christ would be delivered from the bondage of sin through a gospel conversion and enjoy life to the fullest.[47]

When it comes to oikos, understanding the what is the first step toward transforming your church into a gospel conversational church!

Why focus on *oikos*? Upon answering the call of God into fulltime ministry, I was ready to share with those in my circle of influence, that is, my oikos. One of the men was a fellow professing Christian and my mentor in the financial planning business where I worked. After sharing about answering God's call, I vividly remember his words of response as they shot through my heart like a dagger:

"The last thing this world needs is another preacher."

Ouch! Whoever said, "Sticks and stones may break my bones, but words will never harm me" must have been deaf. Those words hurt.

The truth is as long as God still calls preachers, then the world still needs preachers. A more pressing issue is whether or not the church needs another evangelism book, event, program, strategy, tool, or emphasis. Or, does the church simply need to be reminded of what God has already provided?

God has already provided His gospel and our oikos, and He expects all of us to take His gospel to our oikos. Oikos is not another evangelistic program, event, book, emphasis, strategy, or tool. Oikos is a worldview which helps us see the world through the eyes of Jesus. Jesus has given us people who need to hear the gospel from us. Our role is to get the gospel to the ears of the people in our oikos and God's role is to get the gospel to their hearts.

What would happen if each follower of Christ focused on having gospel conversations with his or her "relational worlds"? What could God do if every follower of Christ embraced the truth that God so loved *their* world, *their* oikos, *their* household, that He sent His only Son, Jesus, to save them?

Does reaching one's oikos actually work? One could argue, according to the New Testament, reaching one's oikos was the plan from the beginning.

- ○ **Demon-possessed man** – After Jesus healed the demon-possessed man, He said: "Go home to your own people [oikos] and tell them how much the Lord has done for you, and how he has had mercy on you." (Mark 5:19)
- ○ **Zacchaeus** – When Zacchaeus was saved, Jesus said: "Today salvation has come to this house [oikos]." (Luke 19:9)
- ○ **Son of a royal official** – When Jesus healed the son of a royal official, "...he and his whole household [oikos] believed." (John 4:53)
- ○ **Tax collector turned Jesus follower** – Jesus called Levi (Matthew) to be His disciple: "While Jesus was having dinner, [with] Levi's house [oikos] many tax collectors and sinners were eating with him and his disciples, for there were many who followed him." (Mark 2:15)
- ○ **Cornelius** – Cornelius responded to the gospel conversation had with Peter, and he and his household became believers: "He will bring you a message through which you and all your household [oikos] will be saved." (Acts 11:14)

How fascinating that an *oikos* was the environment in which the first Gentile came to saving faith in Christ! Since that time, oikos remains the most common environment by which people are saved as "95% of all believers give credit to someone in their oikos for leading them to Christ."[48]

So, why focus on oikos? 95% of all believers saying that someone in their oikos led them to Christ is reason enough to focus on connecting your oikos to Christ. To transform your church into a gospel conversational church, the *Why focus on oikos?* question must be replaced with *Why not!*

Who are the ones in your oikos? In an interview with *Willow* Magazine, Guy Kawasaki of MacIntosh Computers while discussing the topic of innovation in ministry, said:

"If you want to be effective, then you have to niche thyself. If you try to reach everyone, you'll reach no one."[49]

Let's stop taking a shotgun approach to reaching the lost and start taking a rifle approach. Let's focus on reaching someone by focusing on the ones in our oikos. What steps must we take if we are going to identify our ones in our oikos?

Take a look at people differently. First, we must adjust the lenses through which we see people. We already have relationships with people we encounter on a regular basis, such as: co-workers, mechanics, hairstylists, grocers, Sonic pellet ice carhops, *my pleasure* Chic-fil-a servers, exercise trainers, child's teachers and coaches, and others. Many of these people provide *us* with a service. But, what if we looked at them as Jesus sees them, that is, for the purpose of providing for *them*? I am so thankful Jesus doesn't see us as we see people. Jesus looks upon us with compassion not disdain. If we are going to follow Jesus, then we must not only go where He went but how He went where He went. We must go as those who are looking to serve and not looking to be served.

Make a list of people frequently. Making a list of people in your oikos must be a frequent priority. Why? Some people come and stay in your oikos, and some people come and leave your oikos. Your oikos will change, and it will grow. Start by listing people who are in your home, family, friends, work, school, etc. Some people in your oikos are lost, and some are saved. Some people in your oikos need to be evangelized by you, and some need your encouragement to go and evangelize others.

TAKE A LOOK AND MAKE A LIST

List at least one person in your home:

_____

_____

_____

List at least one person in your family:

_____

_____

_____

List at least one person among your friends:

_____

_____

_____

List at least one person among your social circles:

_____

_____

_____

List at least one person at work or school:

_____

_____

_____

List at least one person on your social media:

_____

_____

_____

Intercede for your oikos

**"I do not ask for these only, but also for those who will believe
in me through their word, that they may all be one, just as you,
Father, are in me, and I in you, that they also may be in us, so that
the world may believe that you have sent me." John 17:20-21**

**"Christ Jesus is the one who died—more than that,
who was raised—who is at the right hand of God,
who indeed is interceding for us." Romans 8:34**

Jesus interceded for His oikos. Do you realize that Jesus had His own oikos which consisted of these twelve disciples: Simon Peter, John, James, Andrew, Philip, Bartholomew, Thomas, Matthew, James, son of Alphaeus, Thaddaeus, Simon the Zealot, and Judas Iscariot?

Did you know that Jesus' oikos included uneducated fishermen, a tax collector, perhaps a politician, and a thief? Each oikos will be different, but no oikos will be perfect.

Did you know that Jesus spent 73% of His time with the twelve disciples and 27% of His time with the crowds? He was involved in forty-three events with the twelve disciples and seventeen events with the masses.[50]

Did you know that Jesus interceded for His oikos—the twelve disciples—often? In John 17:15,17, Jesus prayed, "I do not ask that you take them (Jesus' oikos) out of the world, but that you keep them from the evil one. Sanctify them [Jesus' oikos] in the truth; your word is truth."

Did you know that Jesus interceded for those in each of His disciples' oikos? Jesus continued praying, in John 17:20, "I do not ask for these [Jesus' oikos] only, but also for those [each of the twelve disciples' oikos] who will believe in me through their word."

Have you ever considered that Jesus' praying for the twelve disciples (His oikos) had such an impact on them that they asked Him to teach them to pray? Why did Jesus' oikos ask Him to teach them to pray rather than teach them to preach, perform miracles, teach, heal, share their faith, or study the Torah? Perhaps Jesus' oikos connected His powerful, spiritual, and impactful life with His prayer life.

At this very moment, just now, as I am writing this section, Dr. Tony Wilson, who pastors White Oak Baptist Church in Chattanooga, TN, just sent me this text:

"Hey, my brother! I hope you're doing well. I just prayed for you. I hope you are enjoying your sabbatical. Have a great day."[51]

Tony is one of the pastors in my oikos and vice versa. We regularly pray for one another and challenge one another to have gospel conversations. Who, in your oikos, are you praying for today?

Jesus is interceding for you and your oikos. Do you realize that Jesus is currently seated at the right hand of God? Jesus being at the right hand of God means that God the Son is as equally God as God the Father and as God the Holy Spirit. So, Jesus has full access to God because He is God!

Did you know that Jesus is praying for you right now? Just like Tony praying for me a few moments ago, Jesus is interceding for us right now. Unlike Tony, who does not pray for me every moment, Jesus never stops interceding for us.

Did you know that Jesus is interceding for your oikos right now? Since Jesus is the same today as He was yesterday, then we know that just as Jesus prayed for each of the twelve disciples' oikos, He is praying for our oikos as well.

Jesus expects you to intercede for your oikos. Jesus never expects us to do that which He didn't do, but He does expect us to deny ourselves, take up our cross daily and follow Him. A large part of following Jesus means thinking of others before you think of yourself. It should come as no surprise, then, that Jesus expects you to intercede for your oikos, not ignore your oikos.

The best line of defense against ignoring your oikos is to pray for your oikos. How is that? In order to pray for your oikos you must think about your oikos. Think about it, when you think about your oikos, your awareness of them and availability to them increases exponentially!

At the end of a recent 5:30 a.m. men's workout known as F3, which is a growing part of my oikos, I had the opportunity to pray over one of the men who shared an urgent prayer need. After I prayed, he was appreciative and shared more details about the situation. Now, I know better how to pray for him and look forward to doing so more often.

If we are going to practice everyday evangelism, then we must pray every day for our entire oikos! Where can we start?

Pray for the good of your oikos. Pray for your oikos' needs. What do they need spiritually, physically, relationally, or emotionally? Yes, pray for their needs, but, also, don't be afraid to boldly intercede for their greatest need, that is, for the goodness and grace of God to be realized in your oikos!

Pray for the growth of your oikos. The growth of your oikos, in part, depends upon your intentionality. Blesseveryhome.com is an effective tool which can help a believer be more intentional in growing his or her oikos through the power of prayer. Each morning I receive an email from blesseveryhome.com which contains a list of the names of five neighbors in my neighborhood. The purpose of the email is to pray over five neighbors each day. Check out blesseveryhome.com for more details.

Pray for gospel conversations with you oikos. Start each day, every day, asking Jesus to give you the opportunity, boldness and compassion to have gospel conversations with your oikos. You know people. Do you know if they know Jesus? If not, why not? Ask Jesus to give you the opportunity to ask them if they know Him.

Pray for your oikos' oikos. We don't need another prayer list already; rather, we need to pray for those who are already listed. Pray over the list of people listed in your contacts on your phone or the Rolodex on your desk. Don't just pray for your oikos, but pray for your oikos' oikos!

Invest in your oikos

"It always costs something to make an investment, but the return on investment will be worth the sacrifice."[52] – Mercer.

Your oikos may not be okay. The visual illustration was blinding. Dr. Randy Davis asked for ten children to join him on the platform. He stated:

"If our evangelism trend in Tennessee continues, then nine out of ten children will enter adulthood without putting their faith in Jesus."[53]

At that point, Dr. Davis moved one child to one side of the platform and left nine children on the opposite side. While pointing at the one child, he said:

"One out of ten children in Tennessee are expected to go to heaven."

Turning toward the nine on the other side, he said, "While nine out of ten children in Tennessee are expected to go to hell."[54]

What an indictment! The fact that so few children in Tennessee are coming to Christ, while still in the home (oikos), suggests that your oikos may not be okay. Church, we must stop ignoring and start investing in our oikos.

Stop ignoring and start investing. In Samuel 24:24, David said, "I will not offer burnt offerings to the LORD my God that cost me nothing." When was the last time we offered the LORD anything that cost us something? Or, when was the last time we offered the LORD something that cost us anything? Investing in anything costs something. Ignoring something or someone costs us little if anything.

In our twenty-first century, First World culture, the church in America is so consumer-minded we expect to get what we want when we want. Investing takes too long. Waiting on anything, much less a return on an investment, is becoming a foreign concept in our get-it-now culture. How can we stop ignoring and start investing?

Give something away daily. Steve Gaines inspired this first step toward seeing people as our Savior sees people. Gaines shared that one of his goals is to give something away every day. He seeks to practice generosity daily.[55]

We are most like God when we give. Our God is a giving God. Each day, let's seek to give something away, and it doesn't have to be money. Get creative with what you give away. We can give away our place in line, a prayer, a compliment, a word of encouragement, a Scripture verse, a testimony, the gospel, or anything else the Holy Spirit gives you to give away.

Simply ask the Holy Spirit, "What would You have me give away today?" Remember, what you give away never goes away! God will use it now and for eternity.

As a pastor, I have tried to teach our church staff the importance of what the Bible says in Acts 20:35, "It is more blessed to give than to receive."

Each time we go out for a staff lunch, I remind them that based upon Acts 20:35, they will be blessed if they pay for my lunch. So far, they have all forfeited that blessing. Seriously, let's seek to give something away daily.

Go our of your way weekly. I love my weekly routine. In fact, if my routine gets messed up, then I am not pleasant to be around. The more I read the Gospels, however, the more I am reminded that Jesus was often interrupted. Often times, Jesus' practice was to go out of His way to invest in His oikos.

In today's digital world, most places of business have access to the internet. Go out of your way once a week by taking your office out of the office. One day a week, study or work at a neighborhood coffee shop. Coffee shops provide a place where people are accustomed to engaging people in conversation. Go out of your way weekly by setting up shop in a coffee shop!

Get out of your comfort zone monthly. Part of investing in our oikos is becoming comfortable at being uncomfortable. In 2 Corinthians 1:3, the apostle Paul wrote, "Praise be to the God and Father of our Lord Jesus Christ, the Father of compassion and the God of all comfort."

God is the God of all comfort, but God doesn't comfort us to make us comfortable. God comforts us so that we can comfort others. God's comfort came to you with the purpose of going to someone else.

Set a goal of getting out of your comfort zone monthly. The only time many believers ever get out of their comfort zone is on a mission trip once a year. We can do better than that! Think about ways you can serve your city or community that is out of your comfort zone. Take some time monthly to serve at a jail, nursing home, children's home, or a homeless shelter.

Invite your oikos

> **"96% of the unchurched are at least somewhat likely to attend church if they are invited."**[56] **– Thom S. Rainer.**

After identifying, interceding for, and investing in our oikos, we are now ready to invite our oikos to come to church and to call on Christ. Unfortunately, recent evangelism and church growth stats are alarming and disturbing:

- ○ **96%** of the unchurched are at least somewhat likely to attend church if they are invited.[57]
- ○ **95%** of all Christians have never won anyone to Christ.
- ○ **80%** of all Christians do not consistently witness for Christ.
- ○ **Less than 2%** are involved in the ministry of evangelism.
- ○ **71%** do not give toward the financing of the Great Commission.[58]
- ○ **47%** of practicing Christian millennials believe that evangelism is wrong because it is "wrong to share one's personal beliefs with someone of a different faith in hopes that they will one day share the same faith."[59]
- ○ **In 1993, 89%** of Christians believed that every Christian has a responsibility to share their faith. **In 2018, only 64%** of Christians believe the same.[60]

Invite your oikos to come to church. When was the last time you invited someone to come to church? Surprisingly, 96% of the unchurched would come to church if invited by the churched. Concerning this 96%, Mercer made the following observation:

"96%! That means, of the 160 million unchurched people in the United States, 154 million of them would be at least somewhat likely to come to church if someone would just invite them—but only 2% of active churchgoers ever do!"[61]

What a tragedy! While 96% of the unchurched would come to church if invited by the churched, only 2% of the churched ever invite the unchurched to church. It's time for the churched to invite the unchurched to church! It's time for you to invite your oikos to come to church!

When you invite your oikos, be invitational, not confrontational. In other words, be sure to invite your oikos to church; don't indict your oikos for not coming to church. Invitations should always be gracious and never grievous. Continue to invite your oikos to church. Never give up on inviting your oikos to church, because you never know when their life may be at the point where they're ready to give in.

Invite your oikos to call on Christ. Lifeway Research, in partnership with the Billy Graham Center for Evangelism, interviewed two thousand unchurched Americans, that is, people who have not attended a worship service in six months. According to the research, the unchurched are very open to a gospel conversation. Thom S. Rainer wrote:

"Almost eight out of ten unchurched Americans would welcome a gospel conversation. Another 12% would discuss it with some discomfort....We can't use the poor excuse that the unchurched really aren't interested in gospel conversations."[62]

The unchurched, unreached and unengaged people in our oikos are not unchurchable, unreachable, or unengagable. Apparently, the people in our oikos are more open to hearing the gospel of Jesus and being invited to church than we often think. Scripture consistently supports the truth that those thought to be unlovable, untouchable, and unforgivable are, on the contrary, lovable, touchable, and forgivable!

After inviting Himself to Zacchaeus' house, Jesus, then, invited Zacchaeus to Himself. In Luke 19:5, Jesus said, "Zacchaeus hurry and come down, for I must stay at your house today." Then, in Luke 19:10, Jesus said, "Today salvation has come to this house, since he also is a son of Abraham."

The word "Today" in verse 9 of Luke 19 highlights the truth that gospel conversations are not seasonal; they can happen anywhere, anyplace and anytime. "Today" speaks of opportunity and emphasizes urgency. Gospel conversations must include a gospel presentation and a gospel invitation. We must invite people to invite Jesus into their life. We must call people to call on Jesus.

Cultivating a gospel conversational culture in your church starts with you having a gospel conversation with those in your oikos! Don't you want your oikos to experience salvation? Don't you know the only way of salvation is by grace alone, through faith alone, in Christ alone?

Explain the gospel of Jesus' death, burial and resurrection. Expound on the truth that our sin separated us from God and left us in a state of brokenness, but God sent Jesus to rescue us. Extend an invitation for your oikos to come to Christ alone, by grace alone, through faith alone.

Make time for this. I can almost hear you asking, "Where will I find the time to do all of this?" Indeed, one of the most common excuses given for ignoring one's oikos is "I don't have time for this." By the way, that is exactly what is it, an excuse! Indeed, one huge barrier to interceding for, investing in, and inviting our oikos to come to church and to Christ is the *time barrier.*

Jay Pathak and Dave Runyon surmised:

> It's vital to take a step back and ask ourselves if we live at a pace that allows us to be available to those who live around us. That doesn't necessarily mean that you must stop everything right now. Instead it's about taking a look at your commitments and being willing to reprioritize to be more present with your close family and friends, as well as make space in your life for those living nearest you.[63]

Are you pacing yourself to be available for others? Or, are you spacing yourself away from others?

Value such a time as this. In Esther 4:14, Mordecai warned Queen Esther that "If you keep quiet at this time, relief and deliverance will rise for the Jews from another place, but you and your father's house [this would be an oikos in the Greek] will perish. And who knows whether you have not come to the kingdom for such a time as this?"

Esther agreed to go to the King on behalf of her father's house (oikos). Should we not be willing to go to King Jesus on behalf of our oikos? Like Esther, we must replace our selfish *I don't have time for this* with a selfless *for such a time as this.*

What does oikos have to do with gospel conversational churches? What would happen if each member of your church reached one person for Christ this year? If each of those people connected with your church, then your church would double. What would happen if each member of your church reached eight to fifteen people (oikos) this year for Christ?

Mercer shared the following helpful illustration: "One of the first things people want to know about High Desert Church is how large a church it is. A typical conversation goes something like this:

'How big is your church?'

'We have a little over 150,000 people?'

(With an incredulous look), 'My goodness, you have 150,000 people in your church?'

'Yes, but 138,000 of them don't attend yet!'[64]

You see those 138,000 people represent the oikos of the each of the church's 12,000 members. Reaching your oikos is the key to transforming your church into a gospel conversational church!

REFLECTION QUESTIONS

- List the name of the people in your oikos. What can you do to grow your oikos?
- Pray for your oikos every day. How will you make praying for your oikos a priority?
- What are some ways you can use your resources to invest in your oikos?
- Are you living at a pace that makes you available to those in your oikos?
- What things have become more important than taking the gospel of Jesus to your oikos?
- What must you start doing and stop doing to avoid ignoring your oikos?

CHAPTER IV

Focusing on the Wrong List

"The crux of the matter lies in motivation, not methods. An individual or a congregation motivated to evangelize will find ways of doing it."[65] – Michael Green

Have more gospel conversations

Mr. Truett Cathy, the late founder of the Baptist bird, the Christian chicken, the fundamentalist foul, the heavenly hen, the persecuted poultry, the raptured rooster, the home of the free-will waffle fries and the Savior's sauce, that is, Chick-fil-A, had a popular saying. Believe it or not, Mr. Cathy's main motto was not "my pleasure." After a speaking engagement at Red Bank Baptist Church and as he was walking out of the building, the last words heard by Mr. Cathy were "Eat more chicken!"

In Philippians 1:12-18, Paul's message can be summed up this way: "Have more gospel conversations!" While focusing on the proclamation of the gospel more than his own persecution because of the gospel, Paul wrote:

> I want you to know, brothers, that what has happened
> to me has really served to advance the gospel, so that it
> has become known throughout the whole imperial and
> to all the rest that my imprisonment is for Christ. And

most of the brothers, having become confident in the Lord by my imprisonment, are much more bold to speak the word without fear.

Some indeed preach Christ from envy and rivalry, but others from good will. The latter do it out of love, knowing that I am put here for the defense of the gospel. The former proclaim Christ out of rivalry, not sincerely but thinking to afflict me in my imprisonment. What then? Only that in every way, whether in pretense or in truth, Christ is proclaimed, and in that I rejoice.

Two observations from this text prove helpful:

First, Paul's proclamation matters more than Paul's persecution. In this text, Paul is not interested in his fellow laborers for Christ knowing *what happened to him*, that is, the specifics of *his persecution because of the gospel.* He is only interested in the brothers knowing *what has happened* as a result of *what happened to him*, that is, *the proclamation of the gospel.*

As followers of Christ, what happens through us (the proclamation of the gospel) is more important than what happens to us (our persecution because of the gospel).

Second, proclamation matters more than motivation. According to Paul, there were two distinct groups of people who were both proclaiming Christ, but they had different motives.

One group was the *empathetic evangelists* as they were preaching Christ from good will. They loved Paul, loved God, loved people and loved the gospel.

The second group was the *envious evangelists* as they were preaching Christ out of envy and rivalry. They were trying to afflict Paul by claiming that his claim of Christ's resurrection was ludicrous. Ironically, in order to make the claim that Paul's claim was wrong, these *envious evangelists* were proclaiming the gospel.

When it comes to the gospel, *what* we proclaim matters more than *why* we proclaim. Still, don't miss the reality that both groups of evangelists recorded in Philippians 1 were motivated as they both had motives.

Motivation is still important. In fact, more motivation, not more methods, is the key to having more gospel conversations. How can we be more motivated to have more gospel conversations? Every follower of Christ should cultivate a list that will motivate him or her to have more gospel conversations!

Focus on writing a list. Writing out lists remains a popular practice. Different types of lists provide preparation for life circumstances and motivation to achieve goals, such as: Amazon book lists, bucket lists, camping lists, contact lists, to-do lists, not-to-do lists, Ebay lists, fantasy football lists, grocery lists, Amazon playlists, pros and cons lists, Amazon shopping lists, Netflix watch lists, Amazon wish lists, and many other lists. Did I mention any Amazon lists? My wife is killing me with the brown truck deliveries!

Some lists are helpful, and some lists are hurtful. Some lists are right, and some are wrong. As you focus on writing a list to have more gospel conversations, be careful not to focus on writing the wrong list. When it comes to having gospel conversations, we all have a list. Are you focused on the wrong list? Don't focus on writing the wrong list!

We all have focused on the wrong list. Back in Chapter II you were introduced to Angela. Angela was the driver of the food delivery service whose GPS went out while trying to deliver my food. As a result, two hours and fifteen minutes after ordering, I met her and picked-up my own food. She said, "This is the first time my GPS has gone out."

Well, I missed a huge opportunity to have a gospel conversation. I could have said, "God's GPS, the Bible, never goes out! The death, burial and resurrection of Jesus guarantees it!"

Why didn't I say that? I was focused on the wrong list. I was focused on being tired, irritated, hungry, and even hangry. Far too many of us believers are focused on a list of reasons why we *can't, won't, shouldn't, or don't have gospel conversations.*

Some of those reasons include:

○ **I am fearful** – We are naturally fearful creatures. When we think about sharing the gospel with another person, we are fearful of being rejected or ridiculed. Jesus promised that we will be rejected and ridiculed, but He also promised that He would never leave us.

- **I don't know enough** – Do you realize that the fishermen Jesus called to follow Him were uneducated men? Yet, they were able to share the gospel powerfully and effectively. All you *have to know* to share the gospel is all you *had to know* to be saved by the gospel. Indeed, all you needed to know to be saved by the gospel is all you need to know to share the gospel. You know enough!

- **I don't know any lost people** – Did you know that the gospel is not only for lost people? Sure, the gospel saves the unsaved, but the gospel is also saving the saved. Sharing the gospel with both the saved and the lost is beneficial. When you share the gospel with saved people it encourages them to go and do likewise.
By the way, you know plenty of lost people. Case in point, have you shared the gospel with every person listed on your phone. Some of them are lost.

- **My testimony isn't powerful enough** – What you mean is your testimony isn't *colorful* enough? Some believers were saved at a young age, and their conversion experience was not as colorful as others, but in no way does that mean it is any less powerful! If you have a testimony of the resurrected Jesus saving you, then you have a powerful testimony.

- **I don't want to offend anyone** – This excuse may have been more excusable years ago, but, guess what, in 2019 everything offends someone and everyone is offended by something. Sharing your faith can't offend anyone any more than they are currently.

- **It's not my responsibility** – Yes. It. Is.

- **I lack an understanding of the gospel** – For a gospel conversation to occur the gospel of Jesus, that is, His death, burial and resurrection, must be presented and an invitation to trust in Jesus extended.

- **I have seen no vision to share the gospel** – For some, their church casts no vision to have gospel conversations.

○ **I don't feel like it** – If you wait until you feel like having a gospel conversation, then you will never have one. How you feel will fail you.

○ **It will cost too much** – Some are too concerned about what it will cost them to have gospel conversations. It will cost, but it will be worth it!

Certainly, this is not an exhaustive list, but it is exhausting enough. Thom Rainer offered the following eye-opening list of nine reasons why Christians fail to evangelize:

○ **Many don't know what "evangelism" is**
○ **We have few evangelistic role models**
○ **Some church members aren't convinced about lostness**
○ **Fear of the unknown halts our efforts**
○ **We've "gotten over" our salvation**
○ **Pastors aren't taking the lead in evangelism**
○ **We don't really know many lost people anyway**
○ **We don't care about non-believers**[66]

Indeed, countless are the list of reasons we give for why we

We all must focus on the right list. Followers of Christ, we all have a list of reasons why we *don't share the gospel*, but what we need to focus on is a list of reasons why we *must share the gospel*! Every believer must cultivate a list of reasons to have more gospel conversations!

In a sermon preached at Long Hollow Baptist Church, Dr. Greg Wilton offered his own list of twelve reasons to share the gospel. Then, he challenged every believer to cultivate his or her own list of reasons. The following list of nineteen reasons to have more gospel conversations was inspired by and adapted from Dr. Wilton's list.

1. God the Father deserves it!

Paul wrote, in Philippians 2:9-11:

> Therefore God has exalted him and bestowed on him the name that is above every name, so that at the name of Jesus every knee should bow, in heaven and on earth and under the earth and every tongue confess that Jesus Christ is Lord, to the glory of God the Father.

Have you ever bragged on your child? Have you ever bragged on your son or daughter for doing his or her best on a particular day at a particular time? As a mom or dad, how does it make you feel when *someone else* brags on *your* child? Guess what! We get to brag on Jesus for being the best of all time and having the name above every name. How it pleases God the Father when we brag about and point people to God the Son. We can never speak of Jesus too much, because we can never speak of Jesus enough!

Can you think of another more deserving of having his or her son bragged about than God the Father? Reason enough to have more gospel conversations is the fact that God the Father deserves it!

2. God the Son demands it!

As recorded in Matthew 28:18, Jesus said:

> All authority in heaven and on earth has been given to me. Go therefore and make disciples of all nations, baptizing them in the name of the Father and of the Son and of the Holy Spirit, teaching them to observe all that I have commanded you. And behold I am with you always to the end of the age.

Dr. Wilton preached, "As a child, sometimes all the motivation I needed for doing something I didn't want to do was my parents, 'Because I said so!'"[67]

Oh yes, sometimes, in the child-parent relationship "because I said so," is enough said! Certainly, Jesus' ""because I said so" is always sufficient! We must not base our obedience to Jesus' command on how well we feel about the situation. How we *feel* will *fail* us. We mustn't call Jesus "Lord, Lord" and fail to do what He says. Chuck Swindoll said: "Whatever we do, we must not treat the Great Commission as the Great suggestion."[68]

Jesus' "I said so" should be reason enough to have more gospel conversations.

3. God the Holy Spirit directs it!

In Acts 1:8, Luke wrote: "But you will receive power when the Holy Spirit has come upon you, and you will be my witnesses in Jerusalem in all Judea and Samaria, and to the end of the earth."

Do you believe that Jesus came and lived a perfect life? Do you believe that Jesus died on the cross? Do you believe that He was buried? Do you believe that Jesus rose from the dead? Do you believe that Jesus sent the Holy Spirit?

If we believe Jesus on all those points, then shouldn't we believe that Jesus is still alive and the Holy Spirit is still working in the hearts of people? Long before we open our mouths and tell people about Jesus, the Holy Spirit has opened their hearts to hear about Jesus.

The Holy Spirit being our Helper is reason enough to have more gospel conversations.

4. God's Word declares it!

In Romans 10:17, Paul wrote: "So faith comes from hearing, and hearing through the word of Christ."

I preach from the English Standard Version of the Bible, but I reference other versions while studying. The best version of the Bible is whatever version you are reading right now. So, keep reading it!

One of the versions of the Bible in my study is full of empty, blank pages. It represents the 2,163 languages across the world that still do not have the Bible in their native tongue. I am so thankful that the one version we don't have in the English language is the Bible full of empty pages.

I am convinced that one of the consequences of the sin at the Tower of Babel is that many languages are still without the Bible. The fact that we have the Word of God in the English language and the fact that faith comes from hearing the Word should be motivation enough for us to have more gospel conversations.

God's Word is reason enough to have more gospel conversations.

5. The gospel is the greatest news!

Peter said, as recorded in Acts 4:20: "Whether it is right in the sight of God to listen to you rather than to God, you must judge, for we cannot but speak of what we have seen and heard."

In a world full of fake news, bad news and no news, the good news of Jesus is the greatest news! Jesus lived a life we could never live, died a death we should have died, was buried and rose from the grave. How can we keep the good news of Jesus to ourselves?

The fact that the gospel is the greatest news is reason enough to have more gospel conversations!

6. People are lost!

Sharing the purpose of why He came, in Luke 19:10, Jesus said: "For the Son of man came to seek and to save the lost."

Zacchaeus just thought that he was looking for Jesus, and he was, but what he didn't realize is that Jesus was looking for him. Zacchaeus may have found the perfect tree from which to see Jesus, but Jesus created that tree knowing He would one day find Zacchaeus in it.

People everywhere are lost. People in cities are lost. People in the country are lost. People in church are lost. People in neighborhoods are lost. People in homes are lost. People in your oikos are like Kate, John Locke, Sayid, Claire, Charlie, Jack, Hugo, Shannon, James, Boone, Mr. Ecko, Desmond, Libby, and Walt; they are LOST!

David Platt wrote: "Every saved person this side of heaven owes the gospel to every lost person this side of hell."[69]

7. People are loved!

John 3:16 reads this way: "For God so loved the world, that he gave his only Son, that whoever believes in him should not perish but have eternal life."

Braydee, our middle-school daughter, uses the word "awkward" an awful lot. Indeed, people are awkward. Do you need proof? Look in the mirror!

Since we're already awkward, let's be even more awkward about something that is worth being awkward about. That is, the love of God. Telling people that God loves them can be awkward; however, the fact that awkward people are loved is reason enough for us to be awkward and have more gospel conversations!

8. People are looking!

The Philippian jailer, in Acts 16:30:32, asked Paul and Silas: "Sirs, what must I do to be saved?"

The Philippian jailer was not keeping Paul and Silas in jail. God was keeping Paul and Silas in jail to reach the jailer. You see, the jailer wasn't jailing Paul and Silas, God was jailing them so they could share the gospel with the jailer and set him free from sin and death.

People in your oikos are watching you as they are looking for something more than this life can offer. As a result, they are paying attention to how you are living your life as a believer. I know what you are thinking, "That is too much pressure on me!"

One of the times when I am not on my best behavior as a believer is behind the wheel. Do you know there are some people who should not be allowed to operate motorized vehicles? Did you know that they all get in front of me on the road? In an effort to cage my road rage, I have a personalized tag that reads GSPLCNV (GoSPeL CoNVersation).

The tag helps keep me on my best (well, maybe just better) behavior behind the wheel. Why? People are looking! Isn't the fact that people are looking reason enough to have more gospel conversations?

9. People are listed!

> Addressing the Ephesian Elders, in Acts 20:20-21, Paul said:
>
> I did not shrink back from declaring to you anything that was profitable, and teaching you in public and from house to house, testifying both to Jews and to Greeks of repentance toward God and of faith in our Lord Jesus Christ.

Paul declared Jesus from oikos to oikos. It's never okay to ignore your oikos, your family household, your peeps, or your circle of influence. How many people listed in your contacts on your phone have you engaged in a gospel conversation?

The undeniable truth that you know people who don't know Jesus is reason enough to have more gospel conversations.

10. Jesus' coming is sure!

Jesus shared this truth in Matthew 24:14: "And this gospel of the kingdom will be proclaimed throughout the whole world as a testimony to all nations, and then the end will come."

A few years ago, President Trump made a last-minute visit to Chattanooga. Some people received this message via mass text from the President: "I am holding one last massive Get Out to Vote Rally in Chattanooga, TN, Sunday. Get free tickets now!"

The coming of President Trump on that day was so sure that his campaign team made tickets available. Infinitely more sure than the coming of President Trump is the coming of the Lord Jesus Christ! What more motivation do we need to have more gospel conversations?

11. Jesus' coming will be seen!

> Jesus continued in Matthew 24:30-31:

> Then will appear in heaven the sign of the Son of Man, and then all the tribes of the earth will mourn, and they will see the Son of Man coming on the clouds of heaven with power and great glory.

Can you believe we get to see the Son of Man coming in all His glory? Sadly, many are prone to lose sight of the fact that we get to see Jesus coming again. Our world is focused on setting its hope of resurrecting the goodness of mankind on the following: the sexual revolution, social justice, social media, gender revolution, that is, human progress.

As a result, too many in our world claim to be socialist (until they get rich), feminist (until they get married) and atheist (until the airplane starts falling).[70] The high point of and the hope for the human race will be the sudden and seen appearance of the Captain of our Salvation on the battlefield!

Jesus' coming being seen should be reason enough to have more gospel conversations!

12. Jesus' coming will be soon!

In Matthew 24:44, Jesus warned: "Therefore you also must be ready, for the Son of Man is coming at an hour you do not expect."

The numbers are staggering. There are at least 11,759 people groups on earth of which 7,076 are unreached with the gospel. The number of people on planet earth who have not been reached with the gospel is a whopping 4.4 billion.

Some of these people could be your neighbors, coworkers, family, and friends. Are they ready for Jesus' coming? Have you asked them? Isn't it time for us to stop arguing about the gospel and start agreeing to share the gospel? Isn't it time for us to stop arguing about the timing of Jesus' Second Coming and start agreeing to share the truth about Jesus' First Coming?

Adrian Rogers said: "When it comes to the exact timing of Jesus' Second Coming, I'm on the Welcoming Committee not the Planning Committee."[71]

Jesus' coming can happen at any moment. Isn't that reason enough to have more gospel conversations?

13. We are at war!

In Ephesians 6:10-11, Paul urged: "Finally, be strong in the Lord and in the strength of his might. Put on the whole armor of God, that you may be able to stand against the schemes of the devil."

According to the 2016 Global Peace Index, only 10 nations in the world are currently not at war. Meanwhile, 57 million refugees are displaced in the world. Moreover, 13.3% of the world's economy is spent on crime and war.[72]

Not only are most nations at war, but all nations, tribes, languages, and peoples are in a spiritual war between light and darkness. Believers, as the light of the world and the salt of the earth, we are on the front lines of this war. In this all-out-war, it's time for someone to turn on the light and pass the salt![73]

The fact that we are at war should be reason enough to have more gospel conversations.

14. We must teach others to share!

One of the most straight-forward Scriptures about discipleship is found in 2 Timothy 2:1-2:

> You, then, my child be strengthened by the grace that
> is in Christ Jesus, and what you have heard from me in
> the presence of many witnesses entrust to faithful men
> who will be able to teach others also.

Having gospel conversations is more than seeing people come to Christ. It's also about teaching those who come to Christ to go and tell others how they can come to Christ. You were taught to share your faith so that you could teach others to share their faith. Who have you taught to share their faith?

The call for us to teach others to share their faith should be reason enough to have more gospel conversations.

15. Satan must be resisted!

Peter knew what it was like to be tempted. In 1 Peter 5:8-9, he wrote: "Be sober-minded; be watchful. Your adversary the devil prowls around like a roaring lion, seeking someone to devour. Resist him, firm in your faith."

Satan is an imposter. Satan is a phony. Satan can't create anything. He can only counterfeit what is already created. Speaking lies is Satan's native tongue. He is the god-father of lies. He is the ancestor of ancestors of lies. The absolute best way to oppose Satan, the father of lies, is to tell people the truth. Open your mouth and oppose the father of lies by sharing the Father of truth.

The opportunity to oppose Satan should be reason enough to have more gospel conversations.

16. Heaven is awesome!

One of the most powerful Scriptures about heaven is found in Revelation 21:4:

> He will wipe away every tear from their eyes, and death shall be no more, neither shall there be mourning, nor crying, nor pain anymore, for the former things have passed away.

Wow! Think about every experience, sorrow, hardship, death, sickness, disease, natural disaster, betrayal, abuse, war, separation, loneliness, desertion, and anything else that has ever brought a tear to any believer's eye. All of that, one day, will be wiped away. Heaven is awesome!

The awesomeness of heaven is reason enough to have more gospel conversations.

17. Hell is awful!

A frightening Scripture for those who will suffer in hell is found in 2 Thessalonians 1:9: "They (those who do not believe the gospel) will suffer the punishment of eternal destruction, away from the presence of the Lord and from the glory of his might."

Do you believe in a literal hell? Dr. Wilton shared that "in some parts of the world the majority of believers, including pastors, don't believe in hell."[74] The Bible says, however, that hell is not only a real place, but it is a real awful place.

Hudson Taylor said:

Would that God make hell so real to us that we can't rest; heaven so real that we must have people there; Christ so real that our supreme motive and aim shall be to make the man of sorrows the man of joy by the conversion to him of men.[75]

How selfish are we to believe in hell and know the way to escape hell, but never share it with those who are headed to hell? By not telling people how hell can be escaped, we are acting as if hell has been erased. Let's not dismiss hell; rather, let us tell people how to miss hell! We should be ashamed for being ashamed of the gospel.

The awfulness of hell should be reason enough to have more gospel conversations.

18. The Work is unfinished!

In 2 Timothy 4:5, Paul instructed: "Do the work of an evangelist, fulfill your ministry."

At the end of Paul's life, he told Timothy that there was work left undone. God is inviting each of us to join Him in doing the work of an evangelist. How exciting!

Have you ever noticed that families on Family Feud rarely choose to *pass*? Most families choose to *play*. When families do choose to *pass*, the host looks at them like something is wrong. God has prepared work for us to do. God is saying enjoy! Don't pass, but play!

Oswald J. Smith said: "We talk of the Second Coming; half the world has never heard of the first."[76]

The unfinished work of having gospel conversations is reason enough to have more gospel conversations.

19. The workers are few!

In Matthew 9:37, Jesus said: "The harvest is plentiful, but the laborers are few."

Even when you don't feel like sharing the gospel, this reason, the workers are few, is great motivation to do so. Simply stated, there are more gospel conversations to be had than there are people to have them. Of course, the gospel will never be heard unless gospel conversations are being had. But, it's also true that gospel conversations will never be had unless there are gospel conversational churches praying for and sending out gospel conversationalists to have them.

The workers being few in number is reason enough to have more gospel conversations.

Why nineteen reasons to have more gospel conversations? Why not ten, twelve, fifteen or twenty reasons? Well, the answer is not a spiritual one.

The reason I chose to make a list of nineteen reasons is because the current year is 2019. In fact, each year I plan on adding an additional reason. So, for example, by the year 2030, I will have thirty reasons to have more gospel conversations in 2030.

The point of this chapter is simple. You must take ownership of your own motivation to have more gospel conversations. Make your own list. Start now!

REFLECTION QUESTIONS

○ What are some reasons why you don't share the gospel?
○ Make your own list of reasons to have more gospel conversations. How will you adapt your list each year?

○ When it comes to being motivated to have more gospel conversations, in what ways can you guard against focusing on a list of reasons to not have more gospel conversations?
○ What is keeping you from teaching others how to share the gospel?
○ How should belief in heaven and hell motivate one to share the gospel?

---•◦•---

CHAPTER V

---•◦•---

Turning From Avoiding Gospel Conversations

"Do the work of an evangelist, fulfill your ministry." 2 Timothy 4:5

Could you open this for me?

On December 12, 2015, I finished the Rocket City Marathon in Huntsville, Alabama, at the age of forty-one. I barely missed the goal of running my first marathon by the age of forty.

Training for a marathon consists of bitterly cold runs, humid and hot runs, early morning runs, mid-afternoon runs, evening runs, late-night runs, short runs, and long runs. Remembering all the training runs is next to impossible; however, there is one training run I will never forget.

We visit my mother-in-law in Mississippi several times each year. The neighborhood where she resides offers a respectable two-mile run out to the main road. One hot, humid, summer morning, I took off on a four-mile run.

Running in the summer humidity of south-central Mississippi is like running in a sauna. As I was running—well, *running* may be a stretch. As I was jogging—well, *jogging* may be a leap. As I was rogging (a combination of running and jogging)—well, *rogging* may be an exaggeration. As I was walking—again, *walking* may even be up for debate. As I was moving, pouring sweat, panting for oxygen, and thirsting for something, anything, in liquid form, it happened.

Although I was moving slowly uphill for the final quarter-mile of a four-mile run, anyone could tell that I was intentionally trying to exercise. Wearing earbuds was clear evidence that I was listening to jogging tunes. Wearing running shorts, a half-marathon t-shirt, and running shoes was clearer evidence that I was attempting to run. Wearing the painful expression on my face was the clearest evidence that I was trying to jog. Being outside in the middle of a hot, humid day, it was plainly obvious that I was exercising.

Blanketed by the blazing sun and looking up from the bottom of the hill, I noticed an SUV coming over the crest. Immediately, the lady driving began to slow down. The next couple of minutes seemed to be right out of a movie as if everything was moving in slow motion.

The SUV pulled further over to my side of the road. It was so close I could feel the cool conditioned air sweep over my face as the driver's side backseat window rolled down. As the refreshing, crisp, cool air enveloped my blistering, red-hot face, an outstretched arm extended from the deep freezer-like coolness of the vehicle.

In the hand of the outstretched arm was a mouth-watering 20-ounce soft drink. The thirst-quenching drink was covered with small drops of ice cascading down the sides and off the bottom of the bottle. The melting drops of ice almost sizzled as it touched down onto the scorching hot Mississippi pavement.

The sweet, middle-aged lady holding the soft drink, as if practiced a thousand times on a track relay team, handed me that cold, enticing, bottle in stride. I looked at her eyeball-to- eyeball and said,

"Thank you."

Being undeniably thirsty, I truly meant it. Before the grateful words left my lips, I heard the two ladies in the front seat say,

"Wait, stop!"

I stopped. The SUV stopped. The lady who handed me the soft drink asked,

"Could you open this bottle for me?"

What?

"Could you open this bottle for me?"

The only thing worse than running in the Mississippi humidity was holding that ice-cold soft drink, only to open it and hand it back to its owner. As the SUV pulled away, I heard the ladies in the front seat laughing and saying,

"He thought that drink was for him!"

Needless to say, I was shocked! At that moment, the pity party began! Feeling sorry for myself, I was thinking out loud:

"Who stops a person from exercising only to ask them to open a crisp, refreshing, ice-cold drink for themselves?"

"Who, in their right mind, sees a person thirsting and in need of something that they have only to keep it for themselves?"

As I was throwing this pity party, suddenly, God the Holy Spirit dropped the hammer on me—not Thor's hammer, but a hammer stronger than Thor's. God spoke louder than audibly as He impressed this on my heart:

"Sam, how many times have you encountered men, women, boys, and girls who were thirsting and in need of the gospel. Yet, you were more focused on what they could do for you or how they could help you, and you kept the living water, the gospel, to yourself?"

Wow! How ashamed I am of the times when I have been ashamed of the gospel!

At that moment, I knew there was only one thing I could do: repent! I turned from the sin of not having gospel conversations and made a commitment to be intentional about engaging people with the gospel in everyday life.

Repent of not having gospel conversations.

Sure, as a pastor I shared the gospel often from the pulpit, at funerals and weddings, visitations and counseling. But, I failed miserably at sharing the gospel in everyday life. Being intentional about engaging in gospel conversations daily with the people God put in my path was non-existent.

God gripped my heart with Paul's words to a young pastor by the name of Timothy. Yes, in 2 Timothy 4: 2, Paul told Timothy, "Preach the Word," and that I was doing. Yet, in 2 Timothy 4:5, Paul also told Timothy, "Do the work of an evangelist, fulfill your ministry," and that I was not doing.

Paul didn't tell Timothy:

Dabble in the work of an evangelist. God is not interested in us dipping our toe in the evangelism waters. He wants us to jump in, swim around, stir up and be stirred by the evangelism waters. If you want the baptismal waters in your church stirred up, then you must be stirred by the evangelism waters! So, jump in! The water is fine!

Debate the work of an evangelist. God has not called us to debate the work of a Calvinist or an Arminianist; God has called us to do the work of an evangelist! It's time we stop arguing about the gospel and start agreeing to share the gospel.

Delegate the work of an evangelist. Every follower of Jesus is called to point people to Jesus. Paul didn't delegate his work as an evangelist to someone else. In Acts 26:1-2, the Bible says, "So Agrippa (King Agrippa) said to Paul, 'You have permission to speak for yourself.' Then Paul stretched out his hand and made his defense: 'I consider myself fortunate that it is before you, King Agrippa, I am going to make my defense today.'"

God gave Paul a platform with King Agrippa. Likewise, God has given you a platform to engage somebody with the gospel. So, you, like Paul, who got King Agrippa, must get *a grip*, repent, and don't delegate to someone else the work of an evangelist that God has given to you!

Delay the work of an evangelist. Do you realize that the only people who can delay the Great Commission is the church? It will never be politically correct to share the gospel, but it is always biblically correct to share the gospel. Randy Davis said it this way: "I am not worried about the day when we can't share the gospel, I am worried about today when we won't share the gospel."[77]

Dodge the work of an evangelist. God never wants us to dodge the work of an evangelist. As a dad of daughters, I dominate my girls in dodge ball. When my girls, Braydee and Belle, were younger, we would often play "tackle ball" in the playroom of our house. Tackle ball is a combination of football, dodge ball, and anything-goes-ball. Basically, I would try to hit them with the ball while they tried to tackle me. Dodging a ball is fun, but dodging the work of an evangelist is fatal!

Disobey the work of an evangelist. Paul told King Agrippa in Acts 26:19, "O King Agrippa, I was not disobedient to the heavenly vision, but declared first to those in Damascus, then in Jerusalem and throughout the region of Judea, and also to the Gentiles, that they should repent and turn to God."

Failing to engage in gospel conversations is an act of disobedience; it is sin. Furthermore, if you never share your faith, never think about sharing your faith, or never desire to share your faith, then, most likely, you do not have faith in Christ. The first act of obedience for you is to repent of your sin, believe on Jesus who died for your sins and rose from the dead, and place your trust in Jesus alone.

Do away with the work of an evangelist. Paul didn't tell Timothy to do away with the work of an evangelist because the times are changing. Times are changing. Think about how quickly change happens. In 2010, most of us never considered that by the year 2020 the number one taxi cab company in the world would not own one cab: Uber. Or, the number one hotel chain would not own one hotel: Airbnb. Or, the number one retailer would not own one retail store: Amazon. Change is happening so rapidly in our world that this very well may happen by 2020.

Of all the changes we face as believers, some things never change. That is, people are sinners, Jesus alone is Savior, faith comes from hearing, and people can't hear the gospel unless someone tells them.

To begin doing the work of an evangelist, we must first repent of not doing the work of an evangelist! First of all, we must repent of not repenting. We must say, "Lord, I am sorry that I am not sorry." Are you sorry that you are not sorry? Start here by asking the Lord to grant you repentance from not repenting.

Then, repent of not having gospel conversations. Four years ago, I repented of not having gospel conversations in everyday life. Some pastors are naturals at being evangelistic. I am not. In fact, everyone who reads this book is most likely more gifted as an evangelist than I am. We must be intentional about having gospel conversations, or they will never happen. Is it work? Yes, engaging in gospel conversations is work, but it works! So, repent of not doing this work and get to work!

Repentance is the posture of a gospel conversational church.

It's not every day when the local Fire Marshall and Channel 3 News visit your home. The call I received from Tonya went something like this:

"Channel 3 News and the Fire Marshall are coming to our house. Do you want to come home?"

My panic-stricken response:

"Wait! What? Do I need to come home? Is the house on fire?"

Then she explained:

"No. The local news station is doing a story on what to do in case of a fire. They are asking the community the question, 'Do you have an escape plan in case of a house fire?'"

Wow! Having the Fire Marshall and a local news outlet coming to our house not because we'd already had a house fire, but to help us develop an escape plan in case of a house fire was a novel idea.

When the Fire Marshall arrived, the subject of his conversation was not small talk, the weather, sports, the latest and greatest news, current events, politics or even his family. The subject of his conversation was an escape plan in case of a fire. He said: "In case of a house fire, everyone in your family needs to get out of the house and meet at the mailbox."

The mailbox, who knew? Unless he told us, we would have never known that the mailbox was the place for the entire family to meet in case of a house fire.

What is the subject of our conversation? Why do we wait to talk about Jesus and heaven until a friend or family member's funeral? Why not talk to the person about Jesus before his or her funeral? We should be telling people the surefire way to escape the fire of hell before they go there!

To overcome the temptation of not engaging in gospel conversations, we must live in a constant posture of repentance. Repentance is the posture of a gospel conversational church; for repentance is a reminder that we need Jesus and other people do as well.

Engaging in gospel conversations and repentance go hand in hand. When we stop sharing Jesus, we stop repenting. When we stop repenting, we stop sharing Jesus. Conversely, when we start sharing Jesus, we start repenting. When we start repenting, we start sharing Jesus.

This chapter's challenge is simple, but not easy: repent and repeat! The first step toward having gospel conversations is to repent of not having gospel conversations. Then, repeat by living in a posture of repentance.

What would happen if every Christ follower in every church repented of not having gospel conversations? We would see a gospel conversational movement sweep across our churches and communities. What would happen if you and I repented of not having gospel conversations? We would see a gospel conversational movement begin. It starts with you and me!

REFLECTION QUESTIONS

- ○ How would you define repentance?
- ○ How would you describe the correlation between repentance and sharing the gospel?
- ○ Explain why you think having gospel conversations is or is not your responsibility.
- ○ What is your greatest obstacle to doing the work of an evangelist?
- ○ Explain a time when God gripped your heart to do the work of an evangelist.

CHAPTER VI

Talking About Gospel Conversations

"Bless the LORD, O my soul, and forget not all his benefits." Psalm 103:2

In Psalm 103, David is found talking to himself as he said, "Bless the LORD, O my soul...." Why was David talking to himself? He was reminding himself to forget none of the LORD's benefits.

Have you ever been caught talking to yourself? Why do we talk to ourselves? One huge benefit or talking to ourselves is that *at least we know someone is listening.*

A new study, however, found that there are tangible benefits of talking to oneself. Namely, "speaking out loud to yourself was found to be a trait of higher cognitive function. Talking to yourself is a sign of intelligence."[78]

During the study, some participants were told to read the instructions quietly to themselves, while others were told to read the instructions aloud. The participants who read the instructions out loud were more concentrated and performed the task more efficiently. The researchers concluded:

> Even when we talk to ourselves during challenging tasks, performance substantially improves when we do it

out loud. The benefits of talking to yourself come from simply hearing oneself, as auditory commands seem to be better controllers of behavior than written ones.[79]

Did you hear that? The benefits of talking to yourself come from simply hearing. Faith really does come from hearing after all. What's more, hearing the gospel of Jesus is the source of faith. Salvation by grace alone, through faith alone, in Christ alone, is made possible by hearing the gospel. What a benefit!

Yes, the fact that salvation is the potential benefit of hearing the gospel is second to none; however, we need not lose sight of the benefits of sharing the gospel. What are some of the benefits you will experience each time you talk about the gospel? At least the following seven benefits can be experienced each time you talk about the gospel:

We get to highlight hope. When Paul was standing before King Agrippa, in Acts 26:4-8, he said:

> My manner of life from my youth, spent from the beginning among my own nation and in Jerusalem, is known by all the Jews. They have known for a long time, if they are willing to testify, that according to the strictest party of our religion I have lived as a Pharisee. And now I stand here on trial because of my hope in the promise made by God to our fathers, to which our twelve tribes hope to attain, as they earnestly worship night and day. And for this hope I am accused by Jews, O king! Why is it thought incredible by any of you that God raises the dead?

Paul could've easily hoped in his highlight reel. Evidenced by his use of "My manner of life from my youth, spent from the beginning among my own nation…," Paul lived the Jewish life better than any other Jew. His reputation was above and beyond. Parents would've looked at their children and said, "Why can't you be more like Paul?" Or, I guess at that time, "Saul." Paul was the most patriotic Israelite in all of Israel.

Paul's life as a Jew, a Pharisee, and a keeper of the Law was unrivaled. Once he met Christ, Paul's focus shifted from *my manner of life* to *my hope.* Furthermore, according to Philippians 3:8, Paul counted his highlight reel as a loss "for the surpassing worth of knowing Christ Jesus *my* Lord."

Did you notice the evolution of Paul's use of the personal pronoun "my"? He went from highlighting *my resume, my reputation, my resolve, and my religion*, to highlighting *my hope and my Lord.* Paul's hope was the resurrection of Jesus, and his Lord was the resurrected Jesus! Paul refused to hope in is his highlight reel.

Life's highlight reels are real. Are you hoping in your highlight reel? We all have a highlight reel featuring our best moments in this life. What is on your life's highlight reel? Do you find your identity, satisfaction, significance, and value in your career, sports, hobbies, education, success, accomplishments, accolades, likes, follows or re-tweets?

Don't find your value, identity, significance, and satisfaction in your best moments in this world, but find them in the moment the Word became flesh in this world! How do we keep from hoping in our highlight reel and keep on highlighting our hope? It's quite simple. Talk about the gospel and talk about having gospel conversations!

How can your church highlight hope? We must look for every opportunity to point people to Jesus. For example, don't rush through baptisms. Baptism is not a get-it-out-of-the-way activity at the beginning of a worship service or an add-on at the end. Baptism presents an incredible opportunity to engage lost family members and friends by highlighting hope in Christ. The Holy Spirit can use the stirring of the baptismal waters to start a gospel conversational movement in your church.

Bonner Creek Baptist Church was the first church God called me to pastor, and it was almost my last! Our first Sunday, an older man greeted Tonya with a kiss. Before I laid hands on him closed-fisted and repeated, I noticed that all of the people were greeting one another with a kiss. Apparently, in South East Louisiana, it is appropriate to greet people with a holy kiss.

When I arrived at Bonner Creek, the church had about ten to fifteen people attending on Sunday mornings. Then, about two months later, a man stopped me after the service and said, "Pastor, I want to be baptized."

I began to talk to him about the gospel. He understood the gospel and had already made a decision to trust Christ, but he had never followed Jesus in biblical baptism. Our attendance the next Sunday doubled as some of his family and friends came to witness his baptism. At the end of that service, two of his family members said, "Pastor, we want to be baptized."

I shared the gospel with them, and they both decided to trust Jesus as their personal Savior. We scheduled their baptism for the very next Sunday. Sunday came, and our attendance nearly doubled again as more family and friends came to witness more baptisms. After that service, a few other people approached and said, you guessed it, "Pastor, we want to be baptized."

Like clockwork, this pattern kept on repeating itself Sunday after Sunday. Needless to say, this first pastorate spoiled me rotten. I thought: "So, this is how it happens. As a pastor, you stand up, open the Bible, share the gospel, and people get saved each week. There's nothing to this pastoring stuff!"

Over the next twelve months at Bonner Creek, there was not a Sunday whereby we didn't baptize somebody. The church grew from ten to fifteen on Sunday morning to over one-hundred as seventy-two people were saved and baptized that first year.

David Platt, who was one of my seminary professors at the time, shared the story in one of our classes and said, "Jesus is still building His church!"

What happened at Bonner Creek? Here's what happened; the church had not seen a baptism in years. So, when we had the first baptism, it was a huge deal. We celebrated! We shared the baptismal candidate's story. We had people share how they had been praying for the candidates' salvations for years. And, of course, we had dinner on the grounds after worship. After celebrating that first baptism with so much energy and effort, we had to celebrate the others in like manner. And we did.

When you have a baptism at your church, take the time to talk about the gospel conversation that led to each baptismal candidate's salvation. By way of a video testimonial or live, have the person or people who shared the gospel with the baptismal candidate either share part of the story or at least stand-up before the baptism. Also, have anyone who prayed for the candidate stand up before the baptism.

Baptism is an incredible opportunity to highlight hope in Christ and to spark a gospel conversational movement in your church!

We get to tell our testimonies. From Acts 26:9-22, Paul shared his testimony with King Agrippa in the following three ways:

Paul talked about life before Christ. In Acts 26:9, Paul wrote, "I myself was convinced that I ought to do many things in opposing the name of Jesus of Nazareth."

Included in those many things were locking the saints in prison, supporting any deaths of the saints, punishing them and trying to make them blaspheme.

Basically, Paul's testimony before he came to faith in Christ could be summed as "I thought I was helping Yahweh by trying to stamp out followers of the Way."

When you tell your testimony, begin by telling others how your life was before you came to Christ. If you came to Christ at a young age, then you may not have a lot of details in this part of your testimony, and that is okay.

Paul talked about how he came to Christ. Paul wasted no time telling King Agrippa how he came to faith in Christ. In Acts 26:13-18, Paul described his conversion experience on the road to Damascus. He wrote:

> At midday, O king, I saw on the way a light from heaven, brighter than the sun, that shone around me and those who journeyed with me. And when we had all fallen to the ground, I heard a voice saying to me in the Hebrew language, 'Saul, Saul, why are you persecuting me? It is hard for you to kick against the goads.' And I said, 'Who are you, Lord?' And the Lord said, 'I am Jesus whom you are persecuting. But rise and stand upon your feet, for I have appeared to you for this purpose, to appoint you as a servant and witness to the things in which you have seen me and to those in which I will appear to you.

As Paul talked about how he came to Christ, it was certainly powerful. In particular, Paul discovered that he wasn't simply persecuting the followers of Jesus; he was persecuting Jesus Himself. Paul's testimony was quite powerful.

I know what some of you are thinking, "Sam, I don't have a powerful testimony like Paul. I grew up in a Christian home and was saved at a young age. I don't have a dramatic conversion experience."

Your testimony may not be as colorful as the testimonies of others, but your testimony in Christ is no less powerful. If you have a testimony of the resurrected Jesus saving you, then you have a powerful testimony!

Paul talked about life since he came to Christ. One simple statement summed up Paul's life since he came to Christ. In Acts 26:22, he said, "To this day I have had the help that comes from God."

Before Paul came to Christ, his testimony was, "I am helping Yahweh." After Paul came to Christ, his testimony was, "I am not helping Yahweh, Yahweh is helping me."

How has your life been since you came to Christ? Talk about how your life is different. Talk about how you now have peace and joy even in the most difficult trials and trouble. Talk about how Jesus has made all the difference in your life. When you talk about how Jesus is your ever-present help in troubling times, you will be helping someone else!

How can your church tell testimonies? Pastors and church leaders, we must capture testimonies and tell them regularly. God still uses lives-changed-by-the-gospel testimonies to change lives with the gospel.

Communicate testimonies in corporate worship. Do you capture people's testimonies and tell them in corporate worship gatherings? Personal interviews, short videos, and sermon illustrations are natural ways to tell testimonies.

Share testimonies in small groups. Do you have a mechanism whereby people in your Life Groups, traditionally called Sunday School, can share their testimonies with one another? Are your life groups taught in a lecture style? Do you offer smaller discipleship groups whereby people can share their personal testimony with one another?

Post testimonies on social media. Utilizing social media to tell testimonies can spark a gospel conversational movement in your church.

Recently, a pastor in rural Mississippi shared that in the first ten years of his pastorate, the church averaged less than one-hundred in worship. Then, he joined Facebook for the purpose of telling people's testimonies of having gospel conversations. Seven years later that same church today is averaging one thousand in worship. The pastor credits this gospel conversational movement to his over five thousand friends on Facebook who have heard, tagged, and told numerous gospel conversational testimonies.

Video testimonials of testimonies. Encouraging followers of Christ in your church to video a sixty to ninety-second testimony of how they came to Christ can spark a gospel conversational movement.

While speaking with a pastor at the 2019 SBC Convention in Birmingham, I discovered a powerful way to capture and share each follower of Christ's testimony. Each member of this pastor's church was encouraged to shoot a short video on his or her own phone. Next, they uploaded the video to the church media team who posted the video on the church website. Then, each person whose video was posted received business cards with a link to their testimony on the church website. As they encounter people in the busyness of everyday life and don't have time "in the moment" to share their testimony, they can hand the person a business card and invite them to hear their story of hope.

Telling salvation testimonies can spark a gospel conversational movement in your church!

We are reminded to repent. In the American church, we don't have to be reminded to argue, belly-ache, complain, grumble, eat, fuss and fight, voice our opinion, be offended, or be offensive. But there is something that we need to be reminded to do: repent.

Whatever happened to repentance? Some of the best ways to reclaim repentance are to talk about how the gospel of Jesus calls people to repentance. Repent of not calling people to repent. Then, call people to repent.

How can your church cultivate a culture of repentance? Jesus came preaching, in Mark 1:15, "The time is fulfilled, and the kingdom of God is at hand; repent and believe in the gospel." In Mark 1:17, immediately after preaching for a decision, Jesus called His first disciples by saying, "Follow me." In regards to cultivating a culture of repentance in the local church, what can we learn from Jesus?

Preach for decisions. Jesus preached for decisions. He called people publicly to follow Him. Why would we not preach for decisions? Why would we not call people to repentance? Why would we not publicly invite people to repent, believe in the gospel, and follow Jesus?

Extend invitations after preaching. Whatever the type, whether it be coming forward, response on printed card, staff connections down front, Next Steps dinner, encourager rooms, responses via text message, taking printed cards to Connect Central, or any other type of invitation, 100% of the Reaching Tour's most evangelistic churches in Tennessee extended an invitation after gospel preaching.[80] After hearing the preaching of the gospel, people must be given the opportunity to respond.

Extend invitations at weddings. No, that is not a misprint. I really did mean *invitations at weddings,* not *invitations to weddings.* People at weddings need to repent! Pastors and wedding officiants, what an opportunity we have to present an explanation of the gospel and extend an invitation to trust Jesus at weddings. Think about all the family and friends who attend weddings. Think about how many of them are lost and far from God. Always give an invitation for people to pray to receive Christ at weddings. I always do.

Extend invitations at funerals. People at funerals need to repent! What better time to consider the reality of one's mortality than at a funeral? Death is fresh on the minds of people at funerals. Why not tell them about the one, Jesus, who was the firstborn from the dead? That is, Jesus was the first to die and be raised from the dead to *never die again.* All who believe in Jesus, although they die, will live for all eternity. What better news could you possibly share! What better place than a funeral!

Reminding people to repent by cultivating a culture of repentance can spark a gospel conversational movement.

We get to remember our release. In Acts 26:18, Paul pointed to the fact that followers of Christ were released "from the power of Satan to God." Satan is cruel and evil. He is the Tempter who tempts us to sin. Then, when we take the bait hook, line, and sinker, he enslaves us to that sin.

Jesus, however, sets us free from Satan's domination and dominion. Each time we preach the gospel, have a gospel conversation, or talk about talking about the gospel, we are reminded of our release from darkness to light, death to life, Satan to God, and hell to heaven.

How Can Your Church Remember Her Release? Pulling up a chair and partaking in the Lord's Supper is one of the most powerful ways to remember our release from Satan to God. Unfortunately, like baptism, the Lord's Supper can suffer the fate of being an add-on at the end of a corporate worship service.

We must take our time as we partake of the Lord's Supper. Why? The Lord's Supper is all about remembering that because of Jesus' death, God remembers our sin no more. Furthermore, each time we partake of the Lord's Supper, we are proclaiming Jesus' death until He comes again at the Second Coming. Therefore, avoid treating the next Lord's Supper like a fast visit through the Baptist bird, the persecuted poultry, the raptured rooster, that's right, Chick-Fil-A's drive thru.

Take your time. Slow down. Focus on the bread as a symbol of Jesus' broken body. Focus on the cup as a symbol of Jesus' blood. As Greg Laurie has said:

> Some people drink to forget as they drown their sorrows
> in the bottle. When we come to the Lord's Table, we
> don't drink to forget our sorrows, we drink to remember
> the Man of Sorrows who removes our sin.[81]

Taking one's time to partake of the Lord's Supper can spark a gospel conversational movement in your church.

We get to focus on forgiveness. Paul's focus shifted to forgiveness in Acts 26:18, when he said, "that they may receive forgiveness of sins." When we focus on forgiveness, we won't forget to forgive.

How can your church focus on forgiveness? When it comes to forgiving one another, forgiveness is tough to get and even tougher to give. So, how can we focus on forgiveness in the local church?

Preach a series on forgiveness. Every week in every worship service at every church, people need forgiveness, and people need to forgive. There is never a wrong time to preach a series on forgiveness.

Explain forgiveness versus reconciliation. Forgiveness only takes one person, while reconciliation takes at least two people. Forgiveness should happen immediately, while reconciliation will most likely take time. When it comes to relationships among people, be sure to explain the difference between forgiveness and reconciliation. Of course, point to the beauty that the gospel always ensures that God is ready for us to be reconciled to Him. He has offered proof through the death, burial, and resurrection of Jesus!

Ask for and give forgiveness. Forgiveness must be given. Always be willing and ready to give forgiveness individually and corporately. Remember, pastors and leaders, we can't expect God's people to do what we never model ourselves.

Focusing on forgiveness can spark a gospel conversational movement in your church.

We get to rejoice in our reward. Why do we cry at funerals and rejoice at weddings? Don't we have this backwards? Shouldn't we cry at weddings and rejoice at funerals? Think about it, the bride and the groom standing at the altar on their wedding day have no idea what's coming! We should weep and wail at weddings.

Meanwhile, why do we solemnly, with tears of sorrow in our eyes, refer to the death of believing loved ones with: "He's gone to be with the Lord," "She's not with us anymore," "He's gone to meet his maker," "She's passed away," "He gave up the ghost," or "She's in a better place." If a believer, our loved ones are not in a "better place," they are in the best place! Rejoice!

Moreover, I have never had a funeral come undone. I have never officiated a funeral of a man or woman who came back from the dead. But, I have officiated too many weddings that ended in divorce.

How can your church rejoice in her reward? Local churches imitate what the leadership celebrates. Pastors and leaders, if we will celebrate what really matters, then God's people will imitate what matters. What should we celebrate in order to cultivate a gospel conversational culture?

Celebrate the gospel. The death, burial and resurrection of Jesus ensures the reward of every believer in heaven. Period. Take the time to celebrate the gospel from the children's ministry to senior adults. Never allow one gathering to pass without a clear and celebratory presentation of the gospel of Jesus.

Celebrate gospel conversations. Whenever you hear about someone having a gospel conversation, share it! You don't have to divulge sensitive information in order to celebrate the fact that God's people are sharing the gospel.

Celebrate gospel conversions. Whenever anyone comes to Christ in your church, everyone in your church ought to shout!

One of the most celebratory Sundays all year at Red Bank Baptist Church is the Sunday devoted to college student baptisms. On this Sunday, college student attendance skyrockets as all of the baptismal candidates invite their friends. When each baptismal candidate's story is shared, the place erupts in applause.

Sadly, this is not the norm; it is the exception. Yet, everyone loves the college baptismal Sunday! Why isn't this celebratory spirit experienced on every baptismal Sunday? It should be! We must celebrate gospel conversions!

Celebrating the gospel, gospel conversations, and gospel conversions can spark a gospel conversational movement.

We get to re-gift the greatest gift. Have you ever re-gifted a gift? Of course, right? Have you ever re-gifted a wanted gift? Of course not, right? Normally, we re-gift unwanted gifts, not wanted gifts.

Paul said, in Acts 26:22, he was proclaiming "...nothing but what the prophets and Moses said would come to pass: that the Christ must suffer and that, by being the first to rise from the dead, he would proclaim light both to our people and the Gentiles."

In other words, Paul is saying that he is re-gifting the greatest gift. He is giving the same gospel message that Moses and the prophets gave. Each time we give someone the gospel, we are re-gifting the greatest gift ever given.

How can your church cultivate a culture of re-gifting the greatest gift? I shudder to think about the number of times the opportunity to re-gift the greatest gift, that is, giving the gospel, has been missed. How can we avoid missing opportunities to re-gift the greatest gift?

Focus on giving not getting. Getting is not a sin; however, Jesus said it is far better to give than to get. We forget about giving when we focus on getting. Let's lead well and give more than we get.

Focus on re-gifting the gospel. Opportunities to re-gift the gospel abound. Nicole was our server on our eighteenth wedding anniversary. She took our order, and we asked how we could pray for her. She said:

"My day job is an architect. I just finished the architectural plans for a big client, but the client doesn't like the plans. He has requested I redraw the plans. Would you please pray that we can come up with something that he likes."

We did pray for her, but I missed a huge opportunity. What should I have said?

"Do you know that God the Creator is the architect of the universe? Do you know that He drew up some perfect plans? But, every one of us told God, 'God, I don't like your plans. I have my own plans.'

Then, we go away from God's plans. The Bible word for 'going away from God' is sin. Sin separates us from God. Yet, God, who is rich in mercy, love, and grace, sent Jesus to rescue us from our sin and brokenness."

Will you please pray that Tonya and I have another opportunity to share the gospel with Nicole?

Talking about the times when you talked about the gospel or missed the opportunity, as I did with Nicole, can spark a gospel conversational movement in your church. Talk about gospel conversations!

REFLECTION QUESTIONS

○ What are some of the obstacles to talking about gospel conversations in your church?

○ What role can you play in helping the leadership remove the obstacles to talking about gospel conversations?

○ Have you shared your testimony with anyone in your church? How can you help your church make the telling of testimonies a priority?

○ Do you believe that calling people publicly to repent and inviting them to follow Jesus is necessary? Explain.

○ Explain a time when you were encouraged by the way a church celebrated the gospel, a gospel conversation, or a gospel conversion.

CHAPTER VII

Teaching a Gospel Conversational Tool

"'What is the best tool to teach people to share their faith?' The answer is...*any of them*!'"[82] Joel Southerland

Why are many children not being taught the most basic of manners? Apparently, parents are no longer teaching children to say:

"Yes, sir!"

"No, sir!"

"Yes, ma'am!"

"No, ma'am!"

Why are parents not teaching their children these manners? It's hard work! From the time a child can speak until he or she is nine to ten years old, or even older, parents must constantly correct them. Teaching children manners is work, but it works!

Teaching One Tool or Multiple Tools

Teaching the local church to have gospel conversations is no less work, but it works. Speaking of the work of leading the church to engage in evangelism, Ed Stetzer wrote:

People need tools or resources that help them to be more evangelistically engaged. Evangelism is not a natural activity—it often needs prompting to grow within a person's life.[83]

Pastors and church leaders who endeavor in this work, often ask this frequently asked question: "Should I train my church with one evangelistic tool or multiple tools? Which approach is most effective?"

So, what is the better approach? Advantages exist for each train of thought. We will consider the benefits of both of these camps below.

At the age of twenty-one, a local pastor walked me through the Roman Road. Under Holy Spirit conviction, I believed the gospel. After confessing my sin to God, I placed my faith alone, by grace alone, in Christ alone. Over the next several months, I was taught to engage in gospel conversations using one tool, the Roman Road. What are the benefits of learning one tool?

New believers need one tool. New believers need an evangelistic tool to build confidence as he or she continues having gospel conversations. One tool helps a new believer grow in having gospel conversations.

One tool is easy to remember. One tool, as opposed to multiple tools, provides the opportunity for a believer to be conversational in a gospel conversation. On the contrary, trying to recall all the different verses and points of multiple tools can quickly move a gospel conversation to a gospel confrontation. What can become more important to the believer is voicing all the verses and points of all the shiny different tools, rather than listening to the other person in the gospel conversation. As such, the gospel dialogue morphs into a gospel monologue.

One tool simplifies church. One tool simplifies the evangelism strategy of a local church. All the people in the church are exposed to the one evangelistic tool.

Randy Davis shared the following illustration about fishing as a young boy:

When I was a boy, my grandfather would take me fishing and we used short worms, longs worms, artificial worms, live worms, crawfish, crickets, and all the other baits in the tackle box. If none of those baits worked, then we used pieces of bread from our sandwiches to try and catch fish.[84]

Multiple evangelism tools, like multiple baits for a fishermen, help believers disciple more fishers of men. Teaching multiple tools is more beneficial for growing disciples, not new converts. Part of the discipleship process is learning to share one's faith and teaching others also. Different people learn and teach in different ways. Some people are visual, some are analytical, and others are just plain blunt.

Matt Queen identified the following evangelistic personalities:

- ○ **The Charging Bull** – The Charging Bull is one who is blunt, no-nonsense and straight to the gospel.
- ○ **The Story Teller** – One who has the Story Teller personality will implement his or her testimony to share the gospel.
- ○ **The Inquisitor** – The Inquisitor utilizes questions to steer a conversation to the point where the gospel can be shared.
- ○ **The Analogist** – An analogist will use current events or circumstances to start a gospel conversation.
- ○ **The Server** – Servers use different types of service to earn an opportunity to share the gospel.
- ○ **The Networker** – The Networker meets and befriends people with the hopes of sharing the gospel.[85]

One evangelistic tool will connect with one personality type better than another. For example, using Queen's personality types above:

- ○ **The Roman Road** – The Roman Road evangelistic tool connects better with an analytical person more than The Story Teller.
- ○ **The 3 Circles** – The 3 Circles tool connects better with a visual person more than The Inquisitor.
- ○ **Evangelism Explosion** – The EE tool connects better with The Charging Bull more than The Server.
- ○ **The Story** – The Story tool connects better with The Story Teller than The Analogist.

Multiple tools, then, provide more opportunity to have gospel conversations with different types of people.

Regardless if one tool is being taught or multiple tools, one of the greatest benefits to teaching any evangelistic tool is summed up well by this California pastor:

> Our primary reason for offering Continuous Witness Training every year is the evangelistic environment it creates. Our people know that the leadership of this church holds evangelism as a high priority. CWT is one way we keep that priority before the people.[86]

Teaching one or multiple tools can spark a gospel conversational movement in your church!

Teaching Tips

While pastoring the past seven years in Chattanooga, a hidden gem in East Tennessee, I have learned that God called my family to Volunteer country. East Tennessee loves the University of Tennessee, that is, "UT." Although I am not a UT fan, living in UT country means no more trouble spelling DeUTeronomy.

The University of Tennessee's legendary quarterback, Peyton Manning, retired from professional football in March of 2016. During his retirement speech, Peyton said,

> When I was drafted by the Colts, Indianapolis was a basketball and a car racing town but it didn't take long for the Colts to convert the city and state of Indiana into football evangelists.[87]

What can Peyton Manning's "football evangelism" teach us about engaging the lost in everyday life?

Out of respect for Number Eighteen's eighteen-year career and in light of the Bible's command to "do the work of an evangelist," I offer eighteen tips as you engage the lost in everyday life and teach others also.[88]

1. Get started

Manning said the decision to play his senior year in Knoxville was "one of the smartest decisions I've ever made." Eventually, Peyton did start playing professional football.

Getting in the game of sharing your faith by engaging the lost in everyday life won't happen until you get started. Get started by having a conversation. Look and listen for a way to connect with a person in a conversation. Through that conversation, ask God to provide a way to guide the conversation to the gospel.

2. Failures are not final

Peyton Manning holds many professional quarterback records, including the rookie record for the most interceptions. Manning's failed reception attempts didn't stop him from delivering the ball.

Maybe you have tried to engage a person with the gospel but failed to communicate the gospel clearly. Perhaps you have tried to engage a person with the gospel, but you were interrupted. Don't give up! Keep delivering the gospel!

3. Remain coachable

Speaking of his National Football League coaches, Peyton said:

> Over my NFL career, I've had five coaches who have helped me become better at my craft and have helped me become a better human being: Jim Mora, Tony Dungy, Jim Caldwell, John Fox, and Gary Kubiak."

His gratitude for his coaches highlights the fact that Peyton remained coachable.

Remaining coachable is critically important as you continue to engage the lost in everyday life. Keep growing more in your faith, so you will keep sharing your faith more.

4. God's Word is our playbook

Can you imagine the number of playbooks Peyton has memorized throughout his career? Of all those playbooks, he referenced 2 Timothy 4:7 in his retirement speech, "I have fought the good fight, I have finished the race, I have kept the faith."

God's Word is our evangelism playbook. Meditate on it! Memorize it! Obey it! Live it! Share it!

5. The game, not the goal, changes

Eighteen years is an extra-long career in the National Football League, considering the average career length is about 3.3 years.[89] Many changes may occur over the course of eighteen years in the game of football, like rule changes and players' safety. Yet, the goal of football never changes. As former NFL coach Herman Edwards ranted: "You play to win the game!"[90]

The way we engage people with the gospel may change, but the message and the goal of the gospel never changes. The goal of engaging the lost in everyday life is to win souls for the glory of God.

6. The mission is greater than the mission's greatest

The sport of football is even greater than one of football's greatest players, Peyton Manning. The Great Commission is the greatest mission for followers of Christ. Making much of the God who made us and the Christ who remade us is our greatest mission as we make disciples. Even the greatest disciple-maker on earth is not greater than the greatest mission under heaven to make disciples.

7. You are not alone

During his retirement speech, Peyton named family, players, coaches, friends, and fans who joined him on his football journey.

At times, following Christ will be lonely, but being lonely is not the same thing as being alone. When you are lonely, remember you are never alone as you share the gospel. Identify someone who can hold you accountable as you share your faith. Ask someone else to invest in your life by praying with you as you engage the lost with the gospel. Invest in another person who needs to be engaging the lost for Christ.

8. Setbacks don't have to set you back

When speaking about the ups and downs in football, Peyton said: "Football has taught me not to be led by obstructions and setbacks…."

Sin is a setback, but sin doesn't have to set you back in sharing Jesus with the lost. Before you sin, resist giving in to that temptation by resting in God's grace. When you sin, repent, and rest in God's grace. Don't allow sin to set you back from engaging the lost; rather, allow God's grace to set you up to engage the lost.

9. Include your family

When I became a New Orleans Saints fan in 1981, Archie Manning, Peyton Manning's dad, quarterbacked the Saints. Peyton's older brother, Cooper Manning, played football. Peyton Manning played football. Eli Manning, Peyton's younger brother, still plays football. The Manning family is a football family.

Is your family a gospel family? Do you involve your family in sharing the gospel of Jesus? As a family, do you talk about the gospel? As a family, do you pray for lost people? As a family, do you host other families in your home for dinner? As a family, do you share the gospel with others? Share your faith as a family!

10. Endure to the end

Endurance is a theme in 2 Timothy as Paul is imploring Timothy to endure to the end by doing the work of an evangelist. Peyton, addressing the timing of his retirement, said: "After eighteen years, it's time." He endured to the end of his football career.

You are never too old to share your faith. You are never too "out of touch" to share your faith. Endure to the end by sharing your faith to the end.

11. Use Your unique personality

God made no two quarterbacks with the same personality. Peyton played using his own personality and no one else's.

No two followers of Jesus have the same personality. The gospel never changes, but the personalities who share the gospel are never the same. Be the best you can be by being all God made you to be in Christ. Share the gospel through your own personality.

12. Share one conversation at a time

Peyton led the Colts to win at least 12 games in seven consecutive seasons. Still, he could only play one game at a time. Jesus, as the Incarnate Word, engaged people one conversation at a time.

Don't be overwhelmed at the vast lostness around you. Combat that lostness by having one gospel conversation at a time. Engage the lost in everyday life one conversation at a time. Ask God to give you opportunity, boldness, and compassion to have at least one gospel conversation each day.

13. God is aware and cares

Peyton closed his retirement speech with this blessing: "God bless all of you and God bless football."

Does God care about football? God absolutely cares about the people involved in football because God is aware of the people involved in football.

God absolutely cares about you engaging the lost in everyday life because God is aware of the people involved. Be encouraged that God is for you, engaging the lost for Him!

14. Finishing doesn't mean you are finished

Peyton left the football field, but he has something left to offer off the football field. He said:

> There's a scripture reading, 2 Timothy 4:7: "I have fought the good fight and I have finished the race. I have kept the faith." Well, I've fought a good fight. I've finished my football race....

Although his football race is over, Peyton's life's race is not over. As a follower of Christ, you never retire from following Christ. If you are still breathing, God is not finished with you!

15. Leave a living legacy

Of Peyton Manning, Tom Brady said: "Congratulations Peyton, on an incredible career. You changed the game forever and made everyone around you better. It's been an honor."[91]

Indeed, Peyton has left a living legacy in the world of football.

In all of creation under heaven, only the souls of men and the Word of God remain forever. Our mission is to share the Word of God with the souls of men. Leave a living legacy by sharing the gospel of Jesus for it lasts forever!

16. Be grateful

Surmising his thoughts about the game of football, coaches, organizations, players, and fans, Peyton declared: "Grateful is the word that comes to my mind." His gratitude for the game shows that Peyton never got over the game.

One of the ways to guard against never getting over the gospel is to express gratitude for the gospel. Are you expressing gratitude for the gospel? Be grateful as you share the gospel. Show that you are grateful when you share the gospel by smiling.

17. Jesus is the Hero of the gospel

Addressing his preparation and work ethic, Peyton shared:

Pundits will speculate that my effort and drive over the past 18 years were about mastery and working to master every aspect of the NFL game. Well, don't believe them. Because every moment, every drop of sweat, every bleary-eyed night of preparation, every note I took and every frame of film I watched was about one thing, reverence for this game.

Peyton's reverence for the game drove the future Hall of Fame quarterback to be his best.

What drives you to be your best? What is your motivation? Jesus is the hero of the gospel. Jesus is the reason we share. Jesus is the reason we engage the lost in everyday life.

18. Have fun

Peyton's official retirement announcement even had a flavor of fun in it as he said: "There is just something about 18 years. Eighteen is a good number, and today, I retire from pro football."

As you continue to engage the lost in everyday life, don't take yourself so seriously. Peyton didn't. Enjoy sharing the joy of Christ with the lost. Have fun engaging the lost in everyday life and teaching others also!

REFLECTION QUESTIONS

○ What tool or tools have you been trained with to share your faith? Share a time when you used a tool to share the gospel.
○ What is your position on learning and teaching one evangelistic tool as opposed to multiple tools?

○ Of the personality types identified in this chapter, describe the one that most matches your personality?

○ Describe a time when you taught someone to share his or her faith using an evangelistic tool.

○ What teaching tip at the end of this chapter most encouraged you? Explain how.

CHAPTER VIII

Targeting a Goal for Gospel Conversations

"I have become all things to all people, that by all means I might save some." 1 Corinthians 9:22

No Corona Allowed on Campus

That early January day in 2004 was not a fun day. Surrounded by family and friends, Tonya and I stood in the driveway of our first home in Richland, MS, preparing to crank up the loaded down U-Haul. All we had known at that time in our nearly three-year marriage was either standing with us or loaded in the U-Haul. We had sold or given away everything else.

We were following Jesus. That is, we were answering Jesus' call on our life to attend New Orleans Baptist Theological Seminary (NOBTS). But, on that day, for all intents and purposes, the focus was on the fact that we were, well, leaving.

Months before that day, we began to tell family and friends what God was doing in our lives. We believed God was calling us to quit our jobs, sell what we could, give away the rest, move to seminary, and pursue a life of vocational ministry. The responses we received were unexpected and seemed unsupportive:

"What are you thinking? Are you really going to leave good jobs, a nice house, family, friends, and your church family?"

"The last thing this world needs is another pastor."

"Sam, you're going back to school? You weren't even a good student when you were in school. You barely got out of school. It took you seven years to get a four-year degree."

The last statement listed above is without a doubt 100% true. Though hard to hear, these responses were couched in the fact that we were moving from two incomes down to zero incomes and one housing payment to two housing payments. What's more, we were doubling all of our financial responsibility with zero income. On moving day, however, the focus was on the fact that we were leaving.

Our plan was to live on the campus of NOBTS, but there was one problem. NOBTS didn't then nor does it now allow Corona on campus. We learned early in the application process that the policy of NOBTS was *no Corona on campus*. See, God asked Tonya to leave her mom, dad, brother, home, church, small group, friends, job and more. I, therefore, was not about to ask Tonya to leave her Corona.

So, we found an apartment in Slidell, LA, that would allow us to have Corona. We left everything behind except for Tonya's Corona. I guess now would be a good time to inform you that Corona was our two-pound Chihuahua. What else would you've associated with Corona? I mean, come on, we are Southern Baptist!

Corona, our two-pound Chihuahua, represented for us all that was familiar. Yet, the ultimate goal in going to NOBTS was not to ensure we had what was familiar, Corona, with us. The goal was to answer God's call. In order to answer God's call, we had to make sacrifices as we left almost all we knew, save Corona.

The ultimate goal of cultivating a gospel conversational culture is not to ensure we hold onto what is familiar, like Corona the dog, but the goal is to answer God's call and obey His command to fulfill the Great Commission. As we think about targeting a goal for gospel conversations, we will consider the following: seeing the goal of gospel conversations and setting a goal for gospel conversations.

See the Goal of Gospel Conversations

What is a gospel conversation? A gospel conversation is a conversation whereby an explanation of the gospel of Jesus is presented, and an invitation to trust in Jesus is extended. A true gospel conversation must contain a presentation of the gospel and an invitation to trust in Jesus.

What is the goal of gospel conversations? The first four books of the New Testament are known as the Gospels. All four of the Gospels are full of gospel conversations. Throughout the Gospels, Jesus has many gospel conversations with men, women, boys and girls, including His disciples, Nicodemus, the Samaritan woman, Mary and Martha, Zacchaeus, the Rich Young Ruler, the Pharisees, Pilate, and even a thief on the cross.

Interestingly, in John 20:30-31, after Jesus had a gospel conversation with doubting Thomas, the Bible says:

> Now Jesus did many other signs in the presence of the disciples, which are not written in this book; but these are written so that you may believe that Jesus is the Christ, the Son of God, and that by believing you may have life in his name.

According to the Gospels, then, the goal of gospel conversations is gospel conversions. Hence, seeing people come to faith in Christ is the goal of having gospel conversations.

According to Jesus, what is the goal of gospel conversations? In Luke 19:10, Jesus said, "For the Son of Man came to seek and to save the lost." The goal of Jesus' first coming was to seek people far from God and bring them near to God. Jesus came to convert the lost and make disciples who make disciples.

Furthermore, John 3:16 reads this way, "For God so loved the world, that he gave his only Son, that whoever believes in him should not perish, but have eternal life."

"Should not perish" is an important piece of this verse. Jesus didn't come to a not-yet condemned world to condemn; He came to an already condemned world to save. So, "should not perish" is important because without Christ we are all perishing!

At the same time, *whoever believes in him* is just as important. One must believe *in Jesus* in order to avoid perishing as the entire reason Jesus came was to rescue those who are perishing.

Even Paul understood the goal of gospel conversations being gospel conversions as he wrote in 1 Corinthians 9:20-23:

> To the Jews I became as a Jew, in order to win Jews. To those under the law I became as one under the law (though not being myself under the law) that I might win those under the law. To those outside the law I became as one outside the law (not being outside the law of God but under the law of Christ) that I might win those outside the law. To the weak I become weak, that I might win the weak. I have become all things to all people, that by all means I might save some. I do it all for the sake of the gospel, that I may share with them in its blessings.

Clearly, the goal of having gospel conversations is seeing gospel conversions. We will do well to not miss this goal. So, how can we ensure that we don't miss *the goal of more gospel conversions?* We must set *a goal for more gospel conversations.*

Set a Goal for Gospel Conversations

Remember, you and I can save no one, but we can share Jesus with anyone. We are not responsible for *saving through gospel conversions*, but we are responsible for *sharing through gospel conversations.*

The remainder of this chapter will challenge you to target a goal for gospel conversations. Below are some examples of different goals you can target for gospel conversations:

Set an individual goal. Each follower of Jesus should set a goal for gospel conversations. Whether it be one conversation a day, two a month, or ten a year, setting an individual goal is paramount.

Set a family goal. Are you competitive? Is your family competitive? Make it fun. Have a competition in your family of setting and achieving gospel conversation goals. Each family should calculate all the individual gospel conversation goals and set a family goal.

Set a Life Group or Sunday School goal. I know people in life groups are competitive. Scott Simmons is one of the most competitive people I know, and he is a life group leader. Be competitive and have fun. One of the best ways to cultivate a gospel conversational culture in your church is to have each life group set a gospel conversation goal for the year.

Set a discipleship group goal. Needless to say, each discipleship group should have a gospel conversation goal. Sharing the gospel and training others to do so is part of the heart of a discipleship group.

Set a church-wide goal – Each church should set an annual gospel conversation goal. 2018 was the first year Red Bank Baptist Church officially set an annual gospel conversation goal. Our goal, as a church, was to engage in 2,018 gospel conversations in 2018. We ended up having just under 2,000 gospel conversations while seeing 154 people converted to Christ. Not only did God add daily those who were being saved, but He also added a second campus, The Point Church at Signal.

What is happening at Red Bank Baptist and The Point Church at Signal is that people are excited to tell other people about their gospel conversations. In other words, the culture of Red Bank Baptist Church and The Point Church at Signal is changing. We are witnessing a culture shift to a gospel conversational church, and it is awesome! We aren't there yet, but we are on our way.

Targeting a goal for gospel conversations can spark a gospel conversational movement in your church!

REFLECTION QUESTIONS

○ Do you agree or disagree with the goal of gospel conversations being gospel conversions? Explain.
○ What value do you see in setting gospel conversation goals?
○ What are the benefits of setting a gospel conversation goal individually and as a family?

○ What part does accountability or reproducibility play in setting gospel conversation goals in Life Groups or Discipleship Groups?

○ Should churches set annual gospel conversation goals? Explain.

CHAPTER IX

Training People to Have Gospel Conversations

"We all know that reps are what make people successful in almost every area of life. Why would we think that we don't need gospel reps?"[92] Jimmy Scroggins

Day-By-Day Conversion of the Vikings

The year was A.D. 793 and the cry from the Christian settlement in Britain was one of desperation: "From the fury of the Northmen, O Lord deliver us!"[93]

The Vikings, also known as the Northmen, invaded Britain and raided monasteries, churches, and Christian settlements bringing merciless, ruthless, and brutal destruction. Yet, over time, the Lord not only delivered the Christians from the Vikings, but He also delivered the Vikings.

One of the most remarkable known stories in the history of Christianity is the conversion of the Vikings. Although it happened slowly, by the year 1200 the Scandinavian countries became thoroughly Christian.

How did these conversions occur? One conversation at a time. The Vikings' conversion happened mostly by day-to-day conversations as they bumped into Christians in the market-place. We can say, then, that the day-by-day gospel conversions of the Vikings happened via day-to-day gospel conversations.

Day-To-Day Conversations by the Church

What are some effective ways we can train the local church to have gospel conversations daily? The following four ways will help train your church to be a day-by-day gospel conversational church.

Train your church. Pastors and church leaders, if you do not make evangelism a priority, then your church won't either. How can you be intentional about evangelism training? Take the opportunity in the pulpit to train your people in a gospel conversational tool as part of your sermon. I even took the time during the Easter sermon to share the 3 Circles on a whiteboard.

Pastors and church leaders, train each generation in your church to have gospel conversations from children to senior adults. Did you know that approximately 25% of annual baptisms in the Southern Baptist Convention come through Vacation Bible School (VBS)?[94] Train your children to share the gospel with other children at VBS. At Red Bank and The Point Church, we train our children to share their faith using the 3 Circles. Then, during snack time at VBS, we provide markers and paper so our kids can share their gospel with other kids. Train your children to share the gospel with other children.

Train every ministry leader to train their volunteers to have gospel conversations. Build gospel conversation training into every area of ministry for all generations. Utilize Wednesday and/or Sunday nights to train people on how to tell their testimony, share the gospel, and engage in gospel conversations.

CAST is a holistic tool I use to train God's people to share the gospel and their testimony through God's story. Over the six-week training, I teach each person how to write out his or her testimony. Each week I pair people up to share their story with one another.

Personal gospel testimonies are tools used to share the gospel, but no person's testimony *is* the gospel. One still must share the death, burial and resurrection of Jesus and call people to repent and trust in Jesus. Training people how to share the gospel in their story is critical!

Pastors and church leaders, remember, when it comes to training people to have gospel conversations, the old adage *practice makes perfect* may not apply, but practice makes perfect sense! Train. Your. Church. To. Get. Their. Reps. In.

Start with gospel conversation starters. How do you move a casual conversation to a gospel conversation? Asking the right questions at the right time is an art. Frankly, when it comes to the art of asking the right questions, I often struggle as an artist. But, there are some questions that can help start a conversation and then move it towards the gospel.

In relation to gospel conversations, William Fay said:

> Asking probing questions is a lot like using a meat thermometer….Now I can't walk around with a thermometer in my hand, asking people, 'Are you cooking?' But I can insert a question into a conversation to try to determine if God is at work and to see if their hearts are open.[95]

Some good questions include:

"What do you do for a living?"

"What are you living for?"

"In what way can I pray for you?"

"Do you ever think about spiritual things?"

"Do you have a church home?"

"What do you believe happens after death?"

Listen well. People talk about what they deem important. Make a connection with them on their turf. Speak their language. I don't mean speak their dialect (though that would be helpful), but speak about and to what they hold dear. The Holy Spirit will lead you to opportunities to have gospel conversations. Be sure you follow His lead. To do so, you must have a clean heart and a close walk with Him.

Set gospel appointments. A gospel appointment is one whereby both parties know that the purpose of the appointment is to talk about the gospel. One of the obvious benefits of a gospel appointment is that the work of moving a conversation to the gospel is done before the appointment. How do you even go about setting a gospel appointment?

I learned an easy way to schedule a gospel appointment from Pastor David Evans. Simply put, schedule a gospel appointment by blaming it all on your pastor!

Tell the person with whom you are setting the appointment that your pastor assigned you the task of sharing your testimony with someone *(every gospel preacher tasks his hearers with this every week simply by preaching the gospel)*. Then, ask the person if they would *help you out* and allow you to share your testimony with them over a cup of coffee.

Blame your pastor! You probably blame him for everything else anyway. I assure you, he won't mind if you blame him for sharing the gospel.

Engage in gospel engagements. Building relationships with people who are far from God is key to being a gospel conversational church. Look for opportunities in your community to engage people. Make heart connections in your community.

Engage Chattanooga is the outreach ministry whereby our church goes into the community for the purpose of building relationships and sharing the gospel. Whether it be a Back-to-School Bash for a local school, feeding a local football team, joining in community parades, or any other opportunity where people gather, we seek to build relationships. Before each outreach, we train our people to meet people, pray for people, and share the gospel with people.

Encouraging other pastors to train their churches in having gospel conversations, Jimmy Scroggins wrote:

> At my church, we practice turning everyday conversations into gospel conversations in church so we can do it out in the real world and do it with people who don't believe. We train people from the pulpit, in small groups, in kids'

classes, in youth groups, in staff meetings, and in one-on-one meetings.[96]

Training people to have gospel conversations can spark a gospel conversational movement in your church!

REFLECTION QUESTIONS

○ Do you agree or disagree that pastors and church leaders must lead the way in cultivating a gospel conversational culture? Explain.

○ How do evangelism and discipleship relate to one another? Explain why you believe or disbelieve that both are necessary.

○ What gospel conversation starters would you add?

○ What are some questions that have helped you steer a casual conversation to a gospel conversation?

○ Is it important to understand that your testimony is not the gospel? Explain.

CHAPTER X

Tracking the Progress of Gospel Conversations

"What doesn't get measured, doesn't get done."[97] Robby Gallaty

Cuz, We Are Family!

Do numbers matter? If so, how much do numbers really matter? Joey Greer, my younger brother, worked on the equipment crew for the New Orleans Saints for a few years including the 2009 Super Bowl season. Who Dat!

During that time, former University of Tennessee standout, Jabari Greer played cornerback for the Saints. Because their last names are spelled exactly the same, Jabari told Joey, "Cuz, we are family!"

From the equipment crew to the GOAT (Greatest Of All Time), that is, quarterback Drew Brees, the Saints organization pays all employees once per week. During Joey's time with the Saints, paychecks were placed in the lockers of players and all other employees every Wednesday. The Saints Payroll Office label the payroll envelopes with each player or employee initial of their first name and their entire last name.

One payday Joey grabbed his payroll envelope, which was labeled *J. Greer*, and drove to the bank on his lunch break. When he arrived at the bank, Joey opened the envelope and made a startling discovery.

His weekly paycheck was written for about $400,000.00 more than his paycheck from the previous week. He was shocked!

Can you imagine how shocked Jabari Greer was when he opened his paycheck for that week? I wonder how Jabari responded as his paycheck was written for about $400,000.00 less than his previous week's paycheck. When we consider the lack of numbers on Jabari's check that week and the abundance of numbers on Joey's check, we can say with confidence that numbers do matter, a lot!

It Counts To Count What Can Be Counted

Everything that counts can't be counted, numbered, or measured, but numbers and measurements still count. The Old Testament book of Numbers is a testament to the importance of numbers.

When it comes to the matter of measuring the current state of evangelism in SBC churches, Johnny Hunt used the following numbers:

> If 10% of our regular Sunday attenders reached one person with the gospel in 2019, then our baptisms would double from 2018.
>
> If 1/6 of our Sunday attenders in SBC churches led one person to Christ, then we would see one million people saved.
>
> 85% of the people ever baptized in any of our churches came to Christ because of one simple invitation.[98]

Roc Collins, commenting on the state of evangelism in the state of Tennessee, reported:

> Statistics indicate there are six million people in Tennessee, but only three million of them have a personal relationship with Jesus Christ. One out of every two people in the state needs to hear the gospel. One out of every two Tennesseans are lost and headed to hell.[99]

How fascinating that with the vastness of lostness on the state and national level, SBC leadership and many churches have adopted the "Who's Your *One?*" challenge. "Who's Your One?" is a challenge to each SBC church and member to identify one person God has put in their life to reach with the gospel.

How much of an impact can reaching one person with the gospel really make? Well, heaven rejoices more over one who is saved than ninety-nine who are already saved. What's more, if every believer in your church reached one person for Jesus, then your numbers would double.

When launching the "Who's Your One?" challenge, SBC President, J.D. Greear said:

> Sometimes we think the only numbers that really matter are the big ones, but it's the single digits that make the difference...it all starts with one...and ultimately the only number that really matters is one. Who's your one?[100]

How will you know which ones in your church have taken the "Who's Your One?" challenge or any other evangelistic challenge without a tracking mechanism in place? But, who's counting? And, who's counting what?

But, Who's Counting?

As a young pastor, I was counseled to never be alone with a person of the opposite sex who was not my bride, Tonya. Also, I was strongly encouraged to stay away from ministry monies at all costs. Guardrails were established early in my ministry to protect against these two most common ways that pastors fall.

Since hearing and heeding that godly counsel, God has given me three women, my wife and two daughters, who *always* ensure that money stays away from me! But, who's counting?

Keeping score is important. Sports teams have no way of knowing who is winning or losing without keeping score. Can you imagine every sporting event you ever witness ending in a tie? What's more, without keeping score, there is no chance of any tiebreakers? How boring!

Keeping score requires some type of scoreboard. Our two daughters, Braydee and Belle, enjoy playing volleyball. This past season there were a few gyms where their teams played that didn't have a scoreboard. Soon enough, the absence of a scoreboard affected how the crowd responded. No one knew how to respond because no one knew the score.

Keeping score requires some type of scorecard. What qualifies as a point or a goal? How does a team score a point or a goal? How does a football team score a touchdown as opposed to a field goal? Which counts for more points: touchdowns or field goals? Do fumbles or interceptions equal points?

Scorecards help teams know how the score is kept and how the contest is won. In fact, entire game plans are devised based upon scorecards.

Should churches keep score? Should churches utilize scoreboards and scorecards? Like it or not, every church keeps some kind of score and uses both scoreboards and scorecards. The difference lies in the type of scorecards each church uses.

I contend that gospel conversational churches must use a non-traditional scorecard for a new scorecard is required. How can we devise a game plan to cultivate an evangelistic and discipleship culture based on traditional scorecards? Sure, counting Sunday attenders, baptisms, and dollars still counts, but gospel conversations, people being sent out, disciples, and discipleship groups also need to be counted. The traditional scorecard offers no place for the latter to be counted.

There are many ways to amend traditional scorecards and scoreboards to include what is necessary to cultivate a gospel conversational culture in your church. Two ways we keep score at Red Bank and The Point Church are listed below.

Tell us about your gospel conversation. At redbankbaptist.org and on our church app we have a "Tell Us About Your Gospel Conversation" survey whereby people can record their gospel conversations. From start to finish, the process takes all of about forty-five to sixty seconds and reads as follows:

○ **Your name (first and last)**

○ **Your personal email address**
○ **Name of person/persons that you shared with (first name will do)**
○ **Where was the location that you shared?**
○ **How many people did you have a gospel conversation with for this entry?**
○ **What did you share? (Select all that apply)** – The options are as follows: (1) I started a spiritual conversation, (2) I shared the gospel, (3) I shared part of the gospel, (4) I shared my testimony, (5) I invited them to church, (6) After sharing, I found out they were already a believer
○ **How many people prayed to receive Jesus Christ as Savior and Lord?**
○ **Have you placed your ping pong ball in the display in the worship center?**

I know what you are thinking, "What does a ping pong ball have to do with a gospel conversation?" We'll get to that to that momentarily. Why do we use such a survey? The reason we use a survey online is twofold:

First, the survey offers a mechanism to help track gospel conversations. We do realize that not all gospel conversations get recorded, but we know some do.

Second, the survey requests the names of the people involved in each gospel conversation. Each week we print off a report listing all the names of people involved in gospel conversations and the names of those they are engaging. In our weekly staff meeting, we pray over all the names. Every week our staff is praying over people who are having gospel conversations.

Ping pong ball Jesus display on display. What do ping pong balls have to do with Jesus? In our Worship Center, we have a Plexiglas display containing white and red ping pong balls. The white ping pong balls represent gospel conversations, while the red ping pong balls represent salvations as a result of gospel conversations.

After a gospel conversation, a person is encouraged to drop a white ping pong ball in the display. Whenever a person trusts Christ as a result of a gospel conversation, then the person who led them to Christ drops a red ping pong ball in the display. A person can request on the survey to have someone else drop a ping pong ball in on their behalf.

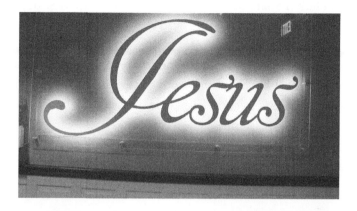

Why do we display ping pong balls? The reason we display ping pong balls is twofold:

The public display of the ping pong balls is a reminder that we set an annual church goal. Each year we empty the display and start over. At the beginning of the year, it is hard to look at an empty display, but at Christmas, it is overflowing!

Every time anyone comes to corporate worship he or she is reminded of what we are all about. Our ping pong public display helps continually reiterate that we exist to connect people to Jesus one conversation at a time.

Tracking the progress of gospel conversations can spark a gospel conversational movement in your church!

Why is sparking a gospel conversational movement so vital?

Two Unlikely Friends

Bailey and Oliver are not friends. Bailey is our family's one-and-a-half-year-old dog we adopted from a local animal rescue center. Oliver is our family's ten-year-old cat that was dropped off at our house years ago by a friend. I know, how much of a *friend* is someone who drops off a cat.

By the way, if you have ever doubted the Fall in Genesis 3, then all you need to do is get a family cat. Before the Fall, God told Adam and Eve to have dominion over "every living thing that moves on the earth." Since the Fall, however, no human being has ever had any dominion over any cat!

Where were we? Oh yeah, Bailey and Oliver do not get along with one another; for they barely tolerate each other. One night these two unlikeliest of friends were brought together by a third party: a small, young rabbit.

As we arrived home that night, Oliver had the wounded rabbit cornered in the garage. I chased Oliver off and retrieved the rabbit. At this point, the rabbit was close to death and died about fifteen minutes later. Oliver killed the rabbit. Belle, our nine year old daughter, was ready to kill the cat.

We explained to Belle that Oliver's nature is that of a predator. He is wired to kill smaller animals. Tonya and I took advantage of this teachable moment. We reminded Belle that Oliver's nature is that of a predator, while our nature is that of sin. We are sinners in need of Jesus, our Savior. Belle's sinful nature didn't subside as she was still ready to kill the cat!

We made a decision not to kill the cat. Instead, we buried the rabbit in the back yard. Belle organized a short service and built a memorial over the tomb of the rabbit. The next day we noticed that the tomb of the rabbit had been disturbed. Upon further investigation, it was determined that Bailey, our family dog, dug up the body and removed the rabbit from the tomb. The tomb of the rabbit is empty! Yes, now we have an empty tomb in our back yard.

Bailey and Oliver have absolutely nothing to do with one another, but now they are forever linked by a dead rabbit who is gone from the tomb. Jesus came to this earth to link together the most unlikeliest of people, who have nothing in common and nothing to do with one another, by bringing them to God. How can we be so sure? His empty tomb proves it!

Most likely, God has placed people in our lives who are not like us and perhaps qualify as the most unlikely of friends. It is highly likely that those people have not believed in the gospel. What an opportunity God has given to us! Let's get to work!

Cultivating a gospel conversational culture in the local church is work, but it works!

May the Lord bless you and keep you and make His face shine upon you and grant you peace as you cultivate a gospel conversational culture in your church.

REFLECTION QUESTIONS

○ How does your church keep score?
○ How would you amend a traditional scorecard to better cultivate a gospel conversational culture in your church?
○ What are some ways your church holds members accountable to evangelism and discipleship?
○ What role does prayer play in cultivating a gospel conversational culture?
○ Does your church have an evangelistic vision? If so, can you articulate that evangelistic vision?

End Notes

1 Chuck Herring, "Does the Church Really Matter?" (sermon based on Matthew 16:13-20 at Collierville First Baptist, preached on February 12, 2017). Accessed 17 July 2019.

2 Barna Group, "51% of Churchgoers Don't Know of the Great Commission" https://www.barna.com/research/half-churchgoers-not-heard-great-commission/ Accessed 19 July 2019.

3 Mark Corbett, "What's so Great about the Great Commission?" http://parresiazomai.blogspot.com/2018/02/whats-so-great-about-great-commission.html. Accessed 19 July 2019.

4 Barna Group.

5 The Babylon Bee, https://babylonbee.com/news/mans-baptism-overturned-after-instant-replay-reveals-he-was-not-fully-submerged. Accessed 23 July 2019.

6 Micah Fries, Sermon at Brainerd Baptist Church.

7 Logos Bible Software 4. Accessed 25 July 2019.

8 Johnston, Thomas P., *Mobilizing a Great Commission Church for Harvest* (Eugene, OR: Wifp & Stock, 2011), 11.

9 Chuck Herring, "Christian Baptism" (sermon at Collierville First Baptist, preached on October 9, 2011). Accessed 26 July 2019.

10 Steve Pearson, *Reaching Tour: What is working in evangelism?* (Franklin, TN: Tennessee Baptist Mission Board, 2018), 4.

11 Pearson, 4.

12 SBC Annual Convention, Annual Reports from NAMB and NOBTS in St. Louis, MO, 2016.

13 Robby Gallaty, "Discipleship Blueprint" Replicate Ministries, 2016.

14 Obid.

15 Dean Inserra, *The Unsaved Christian: Reaching Cultural Christianity with the Gospel* (Chicago, IL: Moody Publishers, 2019), 169.

16 Leon Morris, *The Gospel According to Luke: An Introduction and Commentary* (Grand Rapids, MI: Wm. B. Eerdmans Publishing Com., 1988), 373.

17 Quoted and Adapted from J.D. Greear, "Every Book of the Bible is About Jesus" https://jdgreear.com/blog/jesus-from-genesis-to-revelation/. Accessed on 29 July 2019.

18 Anonymous.

19 Charles Spurgeon, "Quote Fancy" https://quotefancy.com/quote/785340/Charles-H-Spurgeon-A-man-says-to-me-Can-you-explain-the-seven-trumpets-of-the-Revelation. Accessed 29 July 2019.

20 N'dea Yancey-Bragg, "Billionaire Pledges to Pay off $40 million in Student Debt for Morehouse College class of 2019" https://www.usatoday.com/story/news/nation/2019/05/19/billionaire-pledges-pay-off-morehouse-grads-student-loan-debt/3733949002/. Accessed 29 July 2019.

21 Anonymous.

22 Charles Spurgeon, "Good Reads" https://www.goodreads.com/quotes/1091885-when-you-speak-of-heaven-let-your-face-light-up. Accessed 30 July 2019.

23 Michael A.G Haykin. *The Revived Puritan: The Spirituality of George Whitfield (Classics of Reformed Spirituality)* (Dundas, ON: Joshua Press, 2000), 35-37.

24 The Churches Conservation Trust, https://www.visitchurches.org.uk. Accessed 30 July 2019.

25 Ed Stetzer, "No Such Things as 'the Gift of Evangelism'" https://www.christianitytoday.com/edstetzer/2010/july/no-such-thing-as-gift-of-evangelism.html. Accessed 30 July 2019.

26 Obid.

27 Paul McCauley and David Williamson. *Everyday Evangelism: Sharing the Gospel in Conversation* (Kilmarnock, SCT: John Ritchie Publishing, 2018), 24.

28 Matt Queen. *Everyday Evangelism* (Fort Worth, TX: Seminary Hill Press, 2015), 15.

29 Laura Yang. *Everyday Evangelism: Practical Tips to Use Today* (Bloomington, IN: WestBow Press, 2016), x.

30 John Mark Terry. *Church Evangelism: Creating a Culture of Growth in Your Congregation* (Nashville, TN: Broadman and Holman Publishers, 1997), 4.

31 Queen, 70.

32 Yang, ix.

33 McCauley and Williamson, 23.

34 Michael Green. *Evangelism in the Early Church* (Grand Rapids, MI: William B. Eerdmans Publishing Company, 1970), 194.

35 Obid.

36 The list of evangelism modes in the early church were compiled from Green's section on evangelistic methods. Green, 194-235.

37 Jared C. Wilson, *The Gospel Driven Church: Uniting Church-Growth Dreams with the Metrics of Grace* (Grand Rapids, MI: Zondervan, 2019), 150.

38 Barna Group, "2017 Bible-Minded Cities" https://www.barna.com/research/2017-bible-minded-cities. Accessed 31 July 2019.

39 Keith Davy, "The Evangelism Model" https://www.cru.org/us/en/train-and-grow/share-the-gospel/evangelism-principles/the-evangelism-model.html. Accessed 31 July 2019.

40 Obid.

41 Wilson, 151.

42 Gerald Stevens, "Introductory Greek Grammar" https://drkoine.com/lectures/introgk/index.html. Accessed 21 July 2019.

43 Dustin Willis and Aaron Coe. *Life on Mission: Joining the Everyday Mission of God* (Chicago, IL: Moody Publishers, 2014), 24.

44 Tom Mercer, "What is OIKOS?" https://www.tommercer.com/oikos. Accessed 31 July 2019.

45 Tom Mercer. *8 to 15, The World is Smaller Than You Think* (Victorville, CA: Oikos Books, 2009), 20.

46 Logos Bible Software 4. Accessed 1 August 2019.

47 Mercer, *8 to 15: The World is Smaller Than You Think*, 15-16.

48 Mercer, "What is OIKOS?"

49 Guy Kawasaki, "Willow Magazine" interview, Issue 3, 2007.

50 Submitted by Matt Svoboda Executive Pastor of Campus Development at Bridge Church in Nashville, TN. Accessed 1 August 2019.

51 Text Message from Tony Wilson. Received 1 August 2019.

52 Mercer, *8 to 15, The World is Smaller Than You Think*, 99.

53 Randy, Davis, "This Could Be Our Finest Hour" https://baptistandreflector.org/this-could-be-our-finest-hour/. Accessed 1 August 2019.

54 Sermon by Executive Director Randy Davis of the TBMB.

55 Steve Gaines, Speaking at a Retreat in 2017.

56 Thom Rainer, "Ten Surprises About the Unchurched," Christianity Today, November 10, 2004.

57 Mercer, *8 to 15, The World is Smaller Than You Think*, 31.

58 Michael Parrot, "Street Level Evangelism, Where is the Space for the Local Evangelist," Acts Evangelism, 1993.

59 Kate Shellnut, "Half of Millennial Christians Say It's Wrong to Evangelize" https://www.christianitytoday.com/news/2019/february/half-of-millennial-christians-wrong-to-evangelize-barna.html. Accessed 1 August 2019.

60 Barna Group "Sharing Faith Is Increasingly Optional to Christians" https://www.barna.com/research/sharing-faith-increasingly-optional-christians/. Accessed 1 August 2019.

61 Mercer, *8 to 15, The World is Smaller Than You Think*, 31.

62 Thom Rainer, *Thom S. Rainer Growing Healthy Churches. Together*, http://thomrainer.com/2016/12/five-surprising-insights-unchurched/. Accessed 1 August 2019.

63 Jay Pathak and Dave Runyon. *The Art of Neighboring: Building Genuine Relationships Right Outside Your Door* (Grand Rapids, MI: Baker Books, 2012), 43.

64 Mercer, *8 to 15, The World is Smaller Than You Think*, 76.

65 Michael Green. *Evangelism Through The Local Church: A comprehensive guide to all aspects of evangelism* (Nashville, TN: Oliver Nelson,1990), 320.

66 Thom S. Rainer, "Nine Reasons Christians Fail to Evangelize" https://thomrainer.com/2019/08/nine-reasons-christians-fail-to-evangelize/. Accessed 9 August 2019.

67 Greg Wilton,"12 Reasons to Go+Tell" (sermon at Long Hollow Baptist Church preached 8 July 2018) Accessed 2 August 2019.

68 Chuck Swindoll, quote https://www.goodreads.com/quotes/560280-whatever-we-do-we-must-not-treat-the-great-commission. Accessed 2 August 2019.

69 David Platt, *Radical: Taking Back Your Faith from the American Dream* (Colorado Springs, CO: Multnomah Books, 2010), 34.

70 Quote from the Hypocrite Diaries.

71 Adrian Rogers quoted by Steve Gaines https://twitter.com/bellevuepastor/status/817871225913573376. Accessed 2 August 2019.

72 2016 Global Peace Index https://reliefweb.int/sites/reliefweb.int/files/resources/GPI%202016%20Report_2.pdf. Accessed 2 August 2019.

73 Anonymous quote from a SBC leader at SBC Convention 2016.

74 Wilton.

75 James Hudson Taylor https://quotefancy.com/quote/1491403/James-Hudson-Taylor-Would-that-God-would-make-hell-so-real-to-us-that-we-cannot-rest. Accessed 2 August 2019.

76 Oswald J. Smith https://www.goodreads.com/quotes/805691-we-talk-of-the-second-coming-half-the-world-has. Accessed 2 August 2019.

77 Sermon by Executive Director Randy Davis TBMB.

78 Paul Ratner, "Talking to Yourself Out Loud May Be a Sign of Higher Intelligence" https://bigthink.com/paul-ratner/why-talking-to-yourself-out-loud-might-be-just-what-your-brain-needs. Accessed 5 August 2019.

79 Obid.

80 Pearson, 8.

81 Sermon preached at Harvest Christian Fellowship by Greg Laurie.

82 Joel Southerland, "Live on Mission" https://www.namb.net/your-church-on-mission-blog/live-on-mission-evangelism-training. Accessed 6 August 2019.

83 Ed Stetzer, "Strategic Evangelism: Helpful Outreach Tools" https://www.christianitytoday.com/edstetzer/2014/july/strategic-evangelism.html. Accessed 6 August 2019.

84 Randy Davis speaking on the "Listening Tour" for TBMB at Hamilton County Baptist Associational Office on 21 August 2019.

85 Queen, 45-48.

86 Anonymous https://www.namb.net/your-church-on-mission-blog/live-on-mission-evangelism-training. Accessed 6 August 2019.

87 Peyton Manning, Transcript of Peyton Manning's Retirement Speech, http:// www.espn.com/blog/denver-broncos/post/_/id/19274/transcript-of-peyton-mannings-retirement-speech. Accessed 17 January 2017.

88 All of Peyton's following quotes derive from his retirement speech. Peyton Manning, Transcript of Peyton Manning's Retirement Speech, http://www.espn.com/blog/denver-broncos/post/_/id/19274/transcript-of-peyton-mannings-retirement-speech. Accessed 17 January 2017.

89 National Football League Players Association, *Average Playing Career Length in the NFL*, https://www.statista.com/statistics/240102/average-player-career-length-in-the-national-football-league/. Accessed 17 January 2017.

90 Doug Farrar, *10 Years Later*, Herm Edwards' 'You Play to Win the Game!!!' Rant still Resonates, http://sports.yahoo.com/blogs/shutdown-corner/10-years-later-herm-edwards-play-win-game-225650424—nfl.html. Accessed 17 January 2017.

91 Tom Brady, *Tom Brady Congratulates Peyton Manning on Retirement*, https://www.boston.com/sports/new-england-patriots/2016/03/06/tom-brady-congratulates-peyton-manning-on-retirement-you-changed-the-game-forever. Accessed 17 January 2017.

92 Jimmy Scroggins, "Equipping Your Church To Confidently Share The Gospel" https://factsandtrends.net/2017/09/08/equipping-church-confidently-share-gospel. Accessed 7 August 2019.

93 Sermon Illustration "Transforming a Hostile Culture" https://www.preachingtoday.com/search/?query=From+the+fury+&type=. Accessed 7 August 2019.

94 Pearson, 6.

95 William Fay, *Share Jesus Without Fear* (Nashville, TN: Broadman and Holman, 1999), 30.

96 Scroggins.

97 Robby Gallaty, "You Can't Expect what You Don't Inspect" https://replicate.org/you-cant-expect-what-you-dont-inspect. Accessed 7 August 2019.

98 Johnny Hunt, "Ezell Delivers NAMB Report to SBC Messengers" https:// gobnm.com/sbc_news/sbc_annual_meeting/

ezell-delivers-namb-report-to-sbc-messengers/article_832e8e12-93a2-11e9-9b4c-47bec11ac4b4.html. Accessed 7 August 2019.

99 Roc Collins, "The State of Evangelism in Tennessee" https://baptistandreflector.org/the-state-of-evangelism-in-tennessee. Accessed 7 August 2019.

100 J.D. Greear, "Who's Your One?" https://whosyourone.com/?gclid=EAIaIQobChMI2ozb0IHy4wIVj4bACh1ZsgGoEAAYASAAEgLtxPD_BwE. Accessed 7 August 2019.